Preventing Academic Failure

A Multisensory Curriculum for Teaching Reading, Spelling, and Handwriting

Phyllis Bertin
Eileen Perlman

with the assistance of Elizabeth McGoldrick

PAFprogram.com
914-238-4889

ISBN   978-0-9636471-0-8

We thank the many teachers who have inspired, encouraged,

and helped us to constantly improve PAF.

We especially thank

Rachel Bertin and Amy Linden

whose contributions were invaluable.

From the Authors

PAF is a reading program written for teachers, by teachers. It is based on scientific research and over four decades of classroom experience. It may be very different from other reading programs you have used, but for some children it is the only program that will work.

We began our careers as primary teachers in the public schools of New York City and Boston in the 1960s. From the start, we encountered children who puzzled us—children who struggled to read despite their and our best efforts. We tried everything we could think of: different reading programs, lunchtime tutoring, reward systems. Nothing worked, and we were as frustrated as the children.

Later, when studying for our graduate degrees, we were introduced to the emerging field of learning disabilities and a reading methodology called Orton-Gillingham. Orton-Gillingham instruction was designed specifically to be used one-on-one with students with learning disabilities, and it worked!

We immediately saw for ourselves that the key to teaching children with learning disabilities is the right type of instruction. We developed ways to adapt Orton-Gillingham techniques for classroom use, reaching more children effectively, efficiently, and economically. Most important, we realized that if the instruction was introduced in the primary grades, reading failure actually could be prevented. With the encouragement of our school system (we were both together now in New York), we wrote Preventing Academic Failure (PAF) with the hope that regular education teachers would teach all children to read by providing instruction based on Orton-Gillingham techniques in their classrooms.

Each year, we screened kindergarten classes for children who might be at risk for learning disabilities and offered PAF instruction in their regular classrooms. By the fourth grade, 98 percent of these children were reading at or above grade level, and none required special education services. These impressive results were consistent year after year. Soon the program was being replicated in other districts, and we found ourselves both using it and training other teachers.

We have relied on our own teaching experience, the feedback of hundreds of PAF teachers, and the latest scientific research to constantly refine and update the program. We did not invent Orton-Gillingham instruction, but we have written the most comprehensive, effective, and teacher-friendly classroom adaptation available. We are confident you will see amazing results with all your students. Decades after developing PAF, a program that helps every child learn to read, we remain excited and passionate about teaching, because we have found a program that works.

Phyllis Bertin, MS, is a noted lecturer, teacher trainer and school consultant. After teaching mainstream and special education classes, she became the director of special education for the Weston Public Schools, in Connecticut, and then director of education for Windward School, in White Plains, New York. Mrs. Bertin has been a board member of the New York State Branch of the International Dyslexia Association from 1985-1991 and received the Branch Award from the International Dyslexia Association in 1999.

Eileen Perlman, MS, began her career as a classroom teacher and reading specialist and was clinical director of the Reading Initiative Program at the Churchill Center, in Manhattan from 2002-2006. For over thirty years, she was a learning disabilities specialist for the White Plains Public Schools. In addition to her private practice involving diagnosis and remediation, Ms. Perlman is a highly regarded lecturer, teacher trainer, and educational consultant.

Both Mrs. Bertin and Ms. Perlman are fellows of the Academy of Orton-Gillingham Practitioners and Educators and are Dyslexia Therapists certified by the Inernational Dyslexia Association.

If he cannot learn the way we teach,
we had better teach the way he can learn.

Robert Buck

TABLE OF CONTENTS

INTRODUCTION

L earning to read is the most difficult task children face when they first come to school. Some learn to read effortlessly regardless of how they are taught, but about half of school-age children, including the learning disabled, do not learn how to read intuitively. They require a systematic phonics-based program in which reading, spelling, and handwriting are taught as one unified lesson (known as multisensory reading instruction).

Preventing Academic Failure (PAF) fulfills that requirement. It is a comprehensive three-year program for teaching reading, writing, and spelling in the primary grades using multisensory techniques. PAF is designed to prevent reading failure in children with learning disabilities when begun in kindergarten or first grade. It is easier to prevent reading problems than to remediate them. But, it can also be used as an effective beginning reading program for all children and incorporates the reading practices supported by scientific research.

What is multisensory instruction?

Multisensory instruction is a way of teaching reading that integrates reading, spelling, and handwriting into unified lessons. Unlike conventional programs in which these three subjects are taught separately, multisensory programs use a combined approach in which children simultaneously see the letters (visual input), say the letter sounds (auditory input), and write the letters (kinesthetic input). Children read and spell the same material within the same lesson. By strengthening associations and automatic recall, multisensory instruction helps improve word recognition, reading fluency, and comprehension.

Multisensory instruction is based on the work of the physician Dr. Samuel Torrey Orton in the first half of the twentieth century. Dr. Orton was a pioneer in the field of dyslexia, a learning disability that results in reading difficulties. He was among the first to recognize the importance of proper instruction in treating the disorder. The original Orton-Gillingham reading program, developed by Dr. Orton, Anna Gillingham, and Bessie Stillman, was remedial and designed to be used one-on-one with individuals with dyslexia. PAF incorporates the theory and techniques of Orton-Gillingham instruction into an early intervention program intended to be used in schools with groups of children at-risk for reading difficulties.

What are some of the research-based practices in PAF?

PAF incorporates all the instructional practices supported by the latest research. A list of the most important sources can be found in the bibliography. Here are some of the research-based practices that form the foundation of PAF.

✓ **Explicit phonics lessons** in which children are taught to decode and blend sounds into words in order to develop their word recognition skills.

✓ **A sequence of concepts** that progresses from the simplest unit of language (letters) to the most complex (text), with skills practiced and reinforced at each level until they are automatic.

✓ **Oral reading** under the supervision of the teacher that allows children's errors to be monitored and corrected to develop accurate reading. Only when children read accurately can they access the meaning of a text.

✓ **Repeated readings** that provide the practice needed to develop word recognition and fluency.

✓ **Decodable text** that contains only the sounds and words that have been taught, and enables children to apply their word analysis skills in a meaningful context.

✓ **The integration of reading, spelling, and handwriting,** which helps develop the decoding and word recognition skills needed for comprehension.

✓ **Comprehension strategies,** including visualizing, rereading, predicting, paraphrasing, and summarizing, taught under teacher direction.

What kinds of students will benefit from the PAF program?

All beginning readers can benefit from PAF instruction, but for struggling readers, it is critical. Many children start school without an understanding that words can be broken down into sounds (phonemic awareness). Therefore, they cannot learn the first important idea in beginning reading, that each sound in English is represented by a letter or letters (the alphabetic principle). Consequently, decoding and word recognition skills develop slowly, if at all, and without strong word recognition, comprehension suffers. PAF teaches the alphabetic principle, higher-level word analysis skills, and comprehension strategies directly, with sufficient practice and reinforcement to ensure that all children learn to read.

PAF's step-by-step progression leads to an increased sense of mastery and self-esteem. It results in minimum frustration and maximum success for teachers and students.

What are the components of the PAF program?

This teacher handbook is the key to the PAF program. It is your guide to using all the program materials in a sequence of unified lessons. The handbook will tell you which skills to teach, and when and how to teach them. It contains a wealth of information and will soon become your reading bible!

PAF has everything you need for a successful reading program:
- ✓ Card packs for introducing and reviewing skills
- ✓ Word, phrase, and sentence lists for developing accurate and fluent reading
- ✓ Decodable readers and skills books for teaching comprehension
- ✓ Handwriting books for teaching print, cursive, and numerals

Merrill Readers and Skill Books

Stepping Up in Reading Books

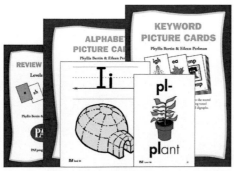

Card Packs

Handwriting Books

How is the handbook organized?

The handbook contains four main sections:

Daily Lesson (pages 5-34)

This section explains the **WHY** and **HOW** of a multisensory lesson. It will help you understand how multisensory instruction is different from other reading programs and how to plan your daily lesson.

Instructional Sequence (pages 35-148)

Beginning on page 35, you will find a 215-level Instructional Sequence that lists **WHAT** skills to teach and **WHEN** to teach them. Each level in the sequence includes specific teaching instructions, information about which pages to use in the PAF materials, and lists of words and sentences to be used for the spelling part of the lesson.

Proficiency Tests (pages 149-180)

This section contains thirteen curriculum-based assessments that are to be administered periodically in order to determine your students' progress and to set instructional goals.

Appendix (pages 181-216)

This section of the handbook contains supplemental information and resources, such as instructions for teaching handwriting, lesson plan forms, sample lessons, and a list of materials. The Rules of Thumb summarizes all the patterns of English that you will teach in the PAF program.

New PAF Reading Series

A new set of readers is being developed by the authors of the PAF program: the PAF Reading Series. The readers follow the PAF Instructional Sequence and can be used in place of the Merrill Readers or for additional decodable text.

Refer to page 216 for further details.

DAILY LESSON

The daily lesson includes the teaching of decoding, comprehension, spelling, handwriting, and grammatical concepts. The sequence of the lesson always remains the same. Each part of the lesson sets the groundwork for the next, beginning with a review of sounds and ending with the teaching of reading comprehension. Here are the five components of the lesson.

1. **Review** (5-10 minutes)
   Children review previously learned sound/symbol associations, nonphonetic words, and suffixes.

2. **Introduction of New Material** (amount of time varies)
   A new concept is taught from one of the following areas:
   - Sound/Symbol Associations (Phonograms)
   - Nonphonetic Words (Red Words)
   - Suffixes
   - Syllable Types and Syllable Division
   - Spelling Rules

3. **Spelling Dictation** (20-30 minutes)
   Children apply the new concept to the spelling of words in isolation and in sentences.

4. **Reading** (45-60 minutes)
   Children read word, phrase, and sentence lists to develop accuracy and fluency. (10-15 minutes)
   Children read decodable text with an adult to develop comprehension skills. (30-45 minutes)

5. **Reinforcement** (amount of time varies)
   Children work independently for additional practice, either at school or at home.

The lesson will take one to one and a half hours in total, but it does not have to be done in one sitting. As you plan your daily schedule, you may intersperse parts of the lesson with other activities. For example, you might do the Review, Introduction of New Material, and Spelling Dictation, send the students to art classes, do Reading, and finally give the students homework for Reinforcement. The sequence of the daily lesson, however, must remain the same.

Each component of the daily lesson will be explained in greater detail, beginning on the following page.

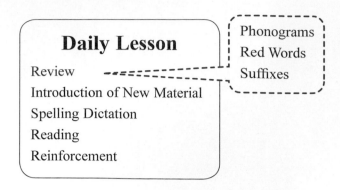

Daily Lesson

Review — — — — — — Phonograms
Introduction of New Material   Red Words
Spelling Dictation   Suffixes
Reading
Reinforcement

Review

Each daily lesson begins with a brief review of previously taught letter sounds (phonograms), nonphonetic words (red words), and suffixes, using Review Pack I.

Separate the review pack into three sets: (1) phonograms, (2) red words, and (3) suffixes. Review each set separately. The review should take no more than ten minutes. Try to establish a routine so that your students know what response you expect without prompting.

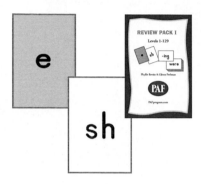

During the review of each set, you will give two different kinds of prompts: (1) a visual prompt, meaning you show the children a card and they say and write their response; and (2) an auditory prompt, meaning you say what is on the card without showing it to the children and again they say and write their response. The children respond exactly the same regardless of the prompt.

Review of Phonograms

A *phonogram* is a written letter or group of letters that stand for a speech sound. For example, the letter *d* represents the sound /d/, the letters *ph* represent the sound /f/, and *igh* represents /ī/*. After each phonogram is introduced, you will place the appropriate card in the phonogram section of the review pack. During the review, the children will practice each phonogram they are learning by associating the letter with its sound and motor pattern (how the letter is formed).

When reviewing phonograms, never use the letter names, because the names do not help in sounding out words.

Children respond to visual prompt (letter form)

Show the phonogram card to the children. Have them respond in unison by saying its sound and *skywriting* simultaneously.

Skywriting means writing the letter in the air using the muscles of the upper arm and shoulder in a full arm swing. To ensure that the large muscles are used, the elbow must be straight and the index and middle fingers extended.

*When you see a letter in slash marks in this handbook, such as /f/, say the sound of the letter, not its name.

Skywriting is an efficient way to do the review. It takes children less time to skywrite than to write on paper. Also, having students skywrite their responses allows you to immediately spot and correct their errors. Because students use their large muscles to skywrite, they are able to feel subtle differences in the formation of letters, such as *b* and *d*. Finally, large muscle memory is very strong. You never forget how to ride a bike or swim. By using large muscles, skywriting helps students remember how to write the letters.

Remember to limit each review to the specific association between the letter form, the sound, and the motor pattern. Students do not need to practice saying the letter names.

Children respond to auditory prompt (letter sound)
Say the sound that appears on an unexposed card. Have the children respond by repeating the sound and skywriting. Finally, show the review card to the class.

Review of Red Words
Red words cannot be sounded out, regardless of the children's level of phonetic proficiency, and simply must be memorized. They are called red words because just as a red traffic light means stop, children must stop at these words, because they cannot be decoded. *Said, was,* and *from* are examples of red words. Since red words cannot be sounded out, **children will say the letter names instead of the letter sounds** during this part of the review; for example, *said, s-a-i-d*.

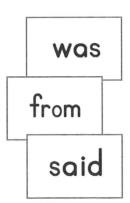

Children respond to visual prompt (word form)
Show the red word card. Have the children respond in unison, saying the word and naming each letter as they skywrite it *(said, s-a-i-d)*.

Children respond to auditory prompt (word name)
Say the word on an unexposed card. Have the children respond in unison by repeating the word and spelling it aloud, naming each letter as they skywrite. Finally, show the class the review card.

Review of Suffixes

A *suffix* is an ending that is added to a word or root to change its meaning, such as *-ing* and *-er.* Suffixes are only reviewed one way, by using their meaning as an auditory prompt. Say the meaning of the suffix on an unexposed card: for example, *Which suffix means* more? Have the children respond by spelling it using the letter names while they skywrite; for example, the children will respond /er/, *e-r.*

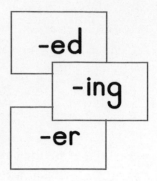

 Your review pack should change in content rather than grow in size. Material that is mastered is replaced by new material. You will periodically give Proficiency Tests to help determine what belongs in the pack.

Daily Lesson	Phonograms
Review	Red Words
Introduction of New Material	Suffixes
Spelling Dictation	
Reading	
Reinforcement	

Introduction of New Material

After the review, the new material for the lesson is introduced. The new material will be a phonogram, red word, syllabication skill, or spelling rule. You will find information about which concepts to teach and in what order to teach them in the Instructional Sequence.

Introduction of a Phonogram

Phonograms are always introduced with a picture of the keyword that containing the new sound. The first phonograms that you will teach are the letters of the alphabet, using the Alphabet Picture Cards.

At the beginning of the program, when you are teaching the individual letters of the alphabet, the introduction of each letter will include instruction on how to write the letter. Handwriting is an integral part of multisensory instruction, because writing letters creates kinesthetic memory of their form. This helps children to read and spell by compensating for auditory and visual memory problems.

Here's what you should do:

• Hold up the picture card and tell the children, *Today we are going to learn how to write the first sound in* fish. *What is the first sound in* fish? A child responds, *The first sound in* fish *is /f/.* Try to avoid adding /ŭ/ to the consonants, as this interferes with blending sounds into words. For example, say /f/, not /fŭh/. Have each child repeat the sound to make sure everyone has the pronunciation correct.

• Give the children the letter name: *This is the letter* f (point to the keyword card) *and the way to write the sound /f/.*

• Demonstrate how to form the letter. You will begin by teaching the lowercase form of each letter, because that is what the children need to learn so that they can read and spell words. The capitals are taught in separate lessons.

In the Appendix, you will find comprehensive instructions on how to teach handwriting. Be sure to read the handwriting section before you begin teaching the program.

- Have the children turn to the large model of the letter in the Handwriting Program for Print book. Be sure the children are facing forward and sitting up straight. Tell them to write the sound, *Write /f/.* Have the children say the sound and "write" it by tracing the model with their index finger several times. The goal is to develop an automatic response between the sound of the letter and the correct motor pattern. Have the children repeat the same procedure several times using a pencil.

- Next, have the children trace the smaller letters on the following page of the handwriting book. Then tell the children to copy the letter using the dots provided as starting points. Finally, have them write the letter on the blank lines.

  In all cases, whether tracing or copying, children must wait for your oral instruction to write the sound, *Write /f/,* and should repeat the sound aloud as they write the letter. The children **should not** do the handwriting book independently; rather, they should work under your continual supervision. In order for their handwriting to improve, they must receive immediate feedback from you after each attempt to write a letter.

- Each page in the handwriting book concludes with a word for the children to copy that is composed of previously taught letters. Some children will need help learning to place the letters in a word close together. Some will need to be taught to use two fingers to help them leave adequate space between words.

After the children have practiced the phonogram in the handwriting book, you will incorporate it into a spelling dictation in the next part of the lesson. Also, you should now place the phonogram into your review pack.

At the beginning of the program, while you are still teaching the letters of the alphabet, you should display the Alphabet Cards in alphabetical order across the front of the room. This should be the only version of an alphabet on display in the room. The children will learn the sounds of the letters more efficiently with only one keyword (*/f/* for *fish*) to remember. You may either put each card on the wall **after** the letter has been introduced or use two sets of the Alphabet Cards, one to display and one to use during the introductory lesson.

Eventually, the new phonograms will contain letter combinations, such as *ee, ar,* and *sh.* By this point, the children will know how to write the individual letters, so there will be no handwriting instruction needed when you are introducing the new phonograms. You will, however, still introduce these phonograms with keywords, using the Keyword Picture Cards. You should then display these cards in place of the alphabet cards.

Introduction of a Red Word

Some days you will teach a red word that the children have to memorize.

Here is what you should do:

• Show a red word using the appropriate card from the review pack. Say, *This is our new red word,* said.

said

• Have a few children use the word in oral sentences to demonstrate that they understand the meaning of the word.

• Have the children say the red word and copy it from the review card, using skywriting and naming each letter as they write *(said, s-a-i-d)*. Saying the letter names while skywriting helps children with poor visual memory memorize these nonphonetic words. Repeat this procedure several times.

• Say the word aloud without showing the card. Have the children repeat and spell the word, saying the letter names as they skywrite once again. Then show the card to the class. Repeat this procedure several times.

In the next part of the daily lesson, you will use the red word in a spelling dictation. Once a red word is introduced, place it in your review pack. Display the red words on a bulletin board so that the children can copy them correctly until memorized.

RED WORDS

STOP

come	off	there
done	one	walk
four	some	want
none	talk	what

Introduction of Suffixes

In PAF, meticulous attention is given to the instruction of suffixes, because understanding suffixes has been proven to enhance word recognition, spelling, vocabulary, and comprehension. The first suffixes you will teach are related to time (*-ing* present tense, *-ed* past tense), quantity (*-s* and *-es* plurals, *-er* more, *-est* most), and possession (*-'s*).

-ing

Here is what you should do:

• Think of questions that will elicit words with the new suffix from the children; for example, *I am standing here right now. What are you **doing**?* (Sitting, thinking, looking.) *What do you hear at the end of all these words*: sit**ting**, think**ing**, look**ing**? The children respond that they hear /-ing/.

• Hold up the suffix card and say, *This is the suffix -ing. We call this the* doing *suffix. It tells us what someone or something is doing.*

• Say *the doing suffix* without showing the card. The children respond *i-n-g,* saying the letter names as they skywrite. Then show the card to the class. Repeat this procedure several times.

In the next part of the daily lesson, you will use the suffix in a spelling dictation. As each suffix is introduced, place the card in your review pack and on a suffix chart.

Suffixes	
-ing	-s
-ed	
-es	
-er	

Level 92

Suffixes	
-ing	-s
-ed	-ful
-es	-less
-er	-ly
-est	
-y	

Level 156

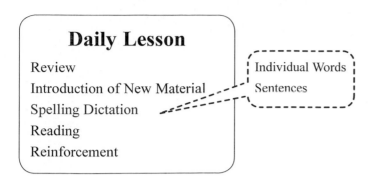

Daily Lesson

Review
Introduction of New Material
Spelling Dictation
Reading
Reinforcement

Individual Words
Sentences

Spelling

After the Review and Introduction of New Material, the newly introduced skill is incorporated into a spelling dictation.

Spelling is a critical tool for teaching reading. In order to spell, children must learn to break words into sounds (phonemic awareness), and become familiar with the letter and letter combinations that represent those sounds (phonics). Learning how to spell improves word recognition and vocabulary, which, in turn, support reading comprehension. In a multisensory program, reading and spelling are taught as reciprocal subjects; children spell and read the same words in one lesson.

Learning disabled children are characteristically poor spellers because of poor phonemic awareness, poor knowledge of letter-sound relationships, difficulty remembering words by sight, and lack of reading experience. The type of spelling program that works best for them is one that includes the direct teaching of phonemic awareness, letter-sound associations, syllable types, and spelling rules in a controlled sequence through the use of spelling dictations.

Spelling is the process of translating a spoken word into its written equivalent (encoding). Dictations allow children to practice encoding words under a teacher's supervision. They provide an opportunity to think and talk about language structure. Children practice spelling words before attempting to read them.

Words and sentences used for dictation are listed in the Instructional Sequence and have been controlled to contain only words that the children can spell based on prior lessons. Select six to nine words and one to three sentences for each dictation, using the lesser amounts for young students who are still learning to write and the larger amounts later in the program. Choose sentences that contain words you have already dictated in isolation.

Dictate Individual Phonetic Words

Spelling with Pocket Chart

Early in the program, you will use a pocket chart each time you introduce a phonogram. Using a pocket chart allows you to model, and children to practice, the breaking of words into sounds for spelling before writing words on paper. Once the students know how to write all the letters of the alphabet, you will stop using the pocket chart and have the students write all the spelling words directly on paper.

Set up the pocket chart by placing letter cards from the Pocket Chart Alphabet in alphabetical order, with all the letters hidden. Put a colored piece of construction paper in the top row of the chart as a background for words you will spell. As you introduce each letter, you will turn over its card and use it to spell new words.

Here is what you should do:

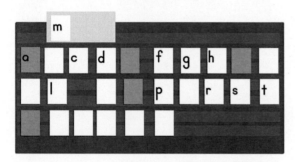

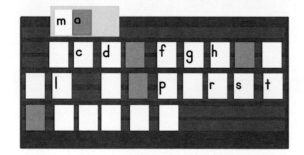

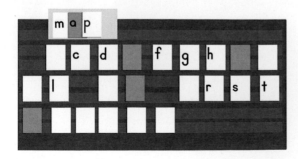

- Call a child to the chart and say a word to be spelled. Use it in a sentence. For example, *map: We made a map of our classroom.*

- Ask the child to repeat the word.

- Have the child isolate the first sound in the word while simultaneously skywriting the letter. Then have him locate the appropriate letter card and place it in front of the construction paper. If he cannot isolate the sound, help him by saying the word while extending the first sound, *mmm -ap.*

- Have the child continue this process for each of the sounds in the word. Overlap the letter cards so that the letters are next to each other.

- Have the child face the pocket chart with his back to the class and lead the children in saying the word, sounding it out while skywriting the word.

- Have the class spell the word on paper, saying the sound of each letter as they write it.

- Spell one or two more words using the pocket chart.

Spelling on Paper

After spelling a few words using the pocket chart, you will dictate more words for the children to write directly on paper. For instructions on specific writing papers to use, see the handwriting section in the Appendix. A dictation is not the same as a spelling test; you must correct each word on every paper before dictating the next one. By the end of each dictation, every word on every paper in the room should be spelled correctly.

Here is what you should do:
- Dictate a word and use it in a sentence; for example, *cut: He has a cut on his finger.*

- Have the children repeat the word.

- At the beginning of the program, model how to say the word sound-by-sound as the children repeat the sounds and write the corresponding letters. Over time, they will begin to automatically sound out words by themselves.

- Walk around the room to check each child's work and give feedback. If a word is spelled correctly, place a check above it. If a word is incorrect, help the child by asking him questions so he can correct his own work. Never correct errors for the children.

Here are some common spelling errors and examples of how to guide the children to make corrections:
- **Vowel substitutions**
  If a child writes *pin* for *pen,* ask: *What vowel sound do you hear in the word* pen?

- **Final consonant substitutions**
  If a child writes *mob* for *mop,* ask: *What is the last sound in the word* mop?

- **Letter omissions**
  If a child writes *let* for *left,* say: *The word is* left. *What letter did you leave out?*

When children have misspelled a word, have them draw a line through the word or put brackets around it and then **write the entire word again**. If a number of children make the same error, ask the children to put down their pencils, and discuss the correct spelling with the entire class. One of the most important parts of dictations is the opportunity to engage your class in conversations about what they are learning. Remember, make sure all the children have spelled the word correctly before dictating the next one.

• Keep track of errors. Analyzing errors will help you determine whether a phonogram or a specific word requires additional practice. You can put any phonograms or red words that are being spelled incorrectly back in your review pack if they have been previously removed.

Dictate Sentences

Having students write dictated sentences provides an opportunity for you to teach punctuation, capitalization, and word spacing.

Here is what you should do:

• Say a sentence using the proper inflection.

• In the beginning of the program, have the children repeat the sentence aloud. Eventually, the children should repeat each sentence silently to themselves.

• Have the children write the sentence on a clean line on their paper. You will probably need to repeat every sentence several times. With short sentences, repeat the whole sentence in one chunk. With longer sentences, you may choose to repeat the sentence phrase-by-phrase. In either case, do not repeat the sentences word-by-word, because children need to practice remembering information in units bigger than individual words. It is helpful to develop a silent signal, such as raising a hand, which children can use to indicate when they need you to repeat a sentence.

• Check each child's work after dictating each sentence. Give positive reinforcement and help children correct their own mistakes. Do not have them rewrite the entire sentence, just the misspelled words.

Here are some common errors and examples of how to guide a child to make corrections:

• **Omitting words**

Read the sentence to me, please. Have the child point to each word as he reads back what he has written. You can teach the children to use carets (^) to write a missing word. Look at Jayden's spelling dictation on the next page for an example.

• **Misspellings**

One of your words is misspelled. See if you can find and fix it. If the child cannot find the misspelled word, point to it and help him self-correct.

• **Errors in punctuation and capitalization**

Are you finished writing your sentence? How would I know? How do we start a sentence?

Sample Dictations

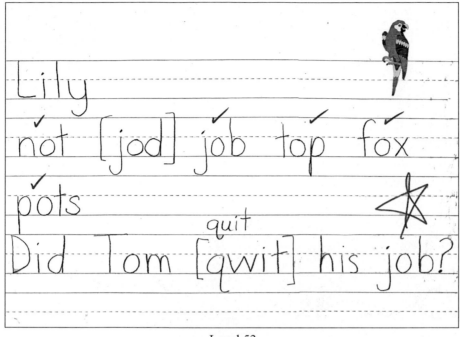

Lily

not [jod] job top fox

pots

quit
Did Tom [qwit] his job?

Level 53

Jayden

keep three (steet) street

queen needed sleeping sweetest

There are three feet in (a) one yard.

Kids need lots of sleep. ☺

Level 145

Carlos   fantastic!

nation station vacation

[polution] pollution fiction

direction

Our nation is over two hundred years old.

Short stories are always fiction.

Oil spills cause water pollution.

Level 205

Divided Dictations

Over time the children may experience areas of confusion that require your special attention. For example, in the beginning of the program children may have difficulty hearing the difference between sounds such as /ĕ/ and /ĭ/. Later in the program they may have difficulty choosing the correct spelling for sounds that have multiple spellings, such as /ā/, which can be spelled *ai*, *a-e,* or *ay.* When these issues arise, give a divided dictation to provide practice making the correct choices. The children divide their paper into columns, and you dictate a mixture of words to be placed in the correct column.

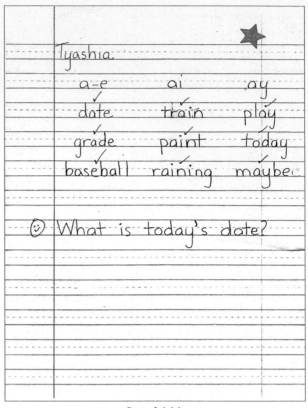

Level 144

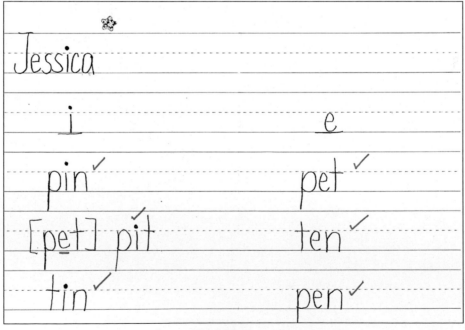

Level 55

Dictations When Introducing a Red Word

The dictation for practicing a newly introduced red word is slightly different from that for practicing phonograms. After the children have written the new red word from dictation several times, dictate three or four sentences using the new word. Dictate fewer sentences for young students who are still learning to write. Do not dictate any individual phonetic words during a red word lesson.

Great job today!

Alex

sure   sure   sure   sure

Those tiger cubs sure are cute.

Their van uses a lot of gas.

They are sure their pet is the cutest one.

Level 138

Excellent

Amy

water   water   water   water

Did you know that water is part of every living thing?

Water turns to ice when it gets very cold.

Swimming and diving are both water sports.

Level 186

PAF

Remember, this is a reading program. You must be sure your spelling dictations do not run into the time allocated for reading even if you do not finish the dictation you have planned.

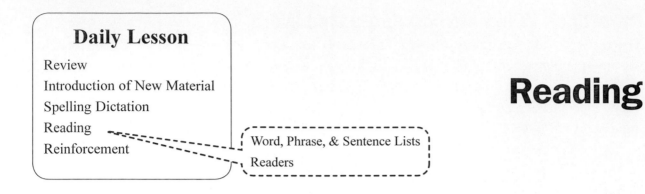

Reading

In the next part of the lesson, reading, the children read aloud to an adult. The reading section has four components:

- **Word, phrase, and sentence lists** for developing accuracy and fluency
- **Text reading** for developing comprehension
- **Repeated Readings** for developing automaticity
- **Reading to children** for developing listening comprehension, vocabulary, and background knowledge

Beginning to read involves forming a link between speech and print. Children must first learn to decode, that is, to associate sounds with letters and blend those sounds into words, and then learn to recognize words automatically. Decoding and word recognition are the foundation of reading comprehension. Without these basic skills, children cannot focus on the meaning of text. Learning disabled children have particular problems developing accurate and fluent reading because of their difficulties with phonologic skills, word retrieval, and visual memory for written words. Therefore, a primary goal of this program is to develop decoding and word recognition.

Decoding and word recognition are best taught using decodable text in which the vocabulary is controlled to contain only previously taught sounds. It is counterproductive to teach children that *a =/ă/* and then ask them to read the words *cake* and *away,* in which the *a=/ā/*. They need reading material in which they can practice their decoding skills and avoid using inappropriate strategies, such as guessing at unfamiliar words. In the PAF program, decodable text is provided in two forms: (1) word, phrase, and sentence lists in the Stepping Up In Reading books; and (2) stories and nonfiction selections in the Merrill Readers and Merrill Skills Books.

When children are learning to read, they need books with decodable text that allows for the application of word analysis skills. The books should repeat the vocabulary from one selection to the next in order to foster word recognition. Phonetic readers, which control vocabulary and present words according to sound patterns, are the most appropriate type of text to use for this purpose.

PAF uses the Merrill Readers, a series of eight phonetic books, because:

- They are consistently phonetic, even at the higher levels.
- They provide more and longer stories than those in most phonetic readers.
- They are well-paced in the introduction of new material.
- They contain both fiction and nonfiction for teaching a variety of comprehension skills.

Book A *(I Can)* focuses on fifteen consonants and the short vowel *a*. It gives you seventy-five pages of text with only one vowel, so your beginning readers will have lots of practice blending sounds into words. You will also introduce the first suffix, *-s*.

Book B *(Dig In)* contains stories with the remaining consonants and the short vowels *i* and *u*.

Book C *(Catch On)* completes the teaching of short vowels with *o* and *e* and introduces digraphs (two letters making one new sound), such as *ch (chin)*.

Book D *(Get Set)* provides additional short vowel practice and all the final consonant blends, such as *-nt* in *bent*.

Book E *(Step Up)* continues the study of short vowels with initial consonant blends, such as *fl- (flag)*.

Book F *(Lift Off)* contains all the common long vowel sounds, such as silent *e (cake)* and vowel teams *(teach)*.

Book G *(Take Flight)* presents the *r*-controlled vowels *(er, ir, ur)*, soft *c* and *g (city, magic)*, and silent letters, such as *kn (knee)*. Some children will transition from this book to chapter books. Others will continue reading in one more Merrill reader.

Book H *(Break Through)* presents the remaining vowel sounds *(oo, au, oi)*. All children now transition to chapter books.

If you are not familiar with PAF, you may at first be surprised by the Merrills. They will probably look different from the books you have seen or used. The Merrills have no pictures and are full of simple stories in familiar settings. Clearly, these are not examples of great literature; rather, the Merrills are a means to an end. They are an instructional tool for teaching the skills necessary to read increasingly difficult texts. The reason that the Merrills have no pictures is so that the children are forced to focus on the print and cannot rely on pictures to guess at unfamiliar words (which is an inefficient reading strategy). The stories are simple because the vocabulary is so carefully controlled.

As your students progress through the Merrills, they will begin to read more interesting and varied texts. In fact, by the time they reach the seventh book in the series (or at any time that they demonstrate proficiency), they will be able to start reading chapter books with great confidence and accuracy.

Reading comprehension is part of every lesson. The goals of teaching comprehension are to improve children's ability to understand information in a particular text and to improve their use of reading strategies that can then be transferred to other reading material. Good readers monitor their comprehension and employ a variety of strategies, such as rereading, to correct misunderstandings. Students benefit from having these strategies taught through direct instruction and modeled by the teacher. Direct instruction is as important in teaching comprehension as it is in teaching decoding.

While the Review, Introduction of New Material, and Spelling portions of the lesson can be done with large groups, it is advantageous to work in smaller groups for reading. This will give each child more opportunity to read aloud under your supervision.

Word, Phrase, and Sentence Lists

Children read lists aloud from the Stepping Up In Reading books under teacher supervision.

Word Lists

Word lists only contain words with previously taught sounds. Children must apply their decoding skills if they do not recognize a word immediately, because the words are in isolation (with no contextual clues). The word lists provide an opportunity to reinforce sound/symbol associations, teach and practice blending sounds into words, and develop word recognition. They provide the repeated practice needed to help children make the transition from deliberate word reading to recognizing words without conscious effort (word recognition).

There are three types of word lists.

Some word lists reinforce a new phonogram, and every word contains the new sound/symbol association. For example, to teach *u=/ŭ/*, the list includes *run, mud,* and *nuts*.

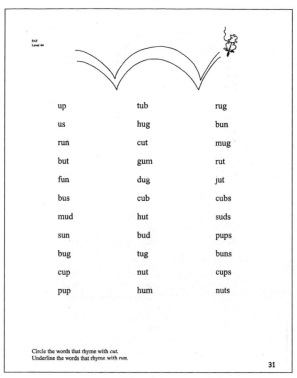

PAF
Level 44

up	tub	rug
us	hug	bun
run	cut	mug
but	gum	rut
fun	dug	jut
bus	cub	cubs
mud	hut	suds
sun	bud	pups
bug	tug	buns
cup	nut	cups
pup	hum	nuts

Circle the words that rhyme with *cut*.
Underline the words that rhyme with *run*.

31

Level 44

Other word lists reinforce previously taught material. For example, after teaching that silent *e* makes a vowel long, the mixed word list would include *care, line,* and *these*.

PAF
Level 139

doze	quote	stale
daze	quite	stole
cape	cave	spoke
cope	cove	spike
sole	tune	grove
sale	tone	grave
wave	cure	fluke
wove	care	flake
these	dime	stroke
those	dome	strike
rude	pale	caring
ride	pole	curing
rode	pile	
mole	lone	dazed
male	lane	dozed
mile	line	
mule		

93

Level 139

Finally, there are word lists that provide practice in reading multisyllabic words. For example, to practice reading words with the suffix *-tion,* the word list would include *nation, fraction,* and *pollution.*

motion	location	subtraction
nation	dictation	injection
lotion	exploration	selection
station	imagination	prediction
vacation	constellation	traction
pollution	addition	friction
celebration	definition	collection
donation	tradition	construction
emotion	condition	direction
conversation	edition	fraction
education	position	affection
communication	composition	caption
operation	action	digestion
transportation	connection	disruption
population	election	mention
rotation	fiction	adoption
revolution	protection	multiplication
infection	consideration	attention

Circle the math words.

105

Level 205

Here is what you should do:

• Read the first column, having each child take a turn reading one word. If a child does not recognize the word, have him decode it by saying the sound of each phonogram and then blending the sounds. If he has difficulty blending the word *cat,* model blending /c/ and /ă/ into /că/, and then adding the /t/ sound to make the word *cat.* Each word must be read as it would be naturally spoken. Tell them, *Read it the way you say it.* The correct pronunciation is necessary to get to the word's meaning.

• Have the children read the list a minimum of two times to provide sufficient practice, more times if needed.

Blending is a difficult skill that must be mastered if children are to become fluent readers. Initially, however, it can be a slow, sound-by-sound process. While children are first learning to blend, extra time should be spent rereading the word lists. Gradually, after much daily practice, children will move from letter-by-letter decoding to word recognition.

Do not use the word lists as vocabulary lessons. Children will not learn the meaning of new words when they are out of context, as they are on the word lists. If a child asks for the meaning of a word, define the word briefly and continue reading the list. It is more effective to address vocabulary while the children are reading the Merrills, while you are reading aloud to the class, or in content area classes, such as science or social studies.

Words introduced on the word lists are reinforced in phrase and sentence lists. Poor readers are often not fluent, instead they read word-by-word. These lists provide practice reading text in meaningful units, provide examples of proper word usage, and enhance both fluency and comprehension.

Explain to students that the word combinations on the phrase lists are only parts of sentences and therefore lack punctuation. Tell them that the purpose of reading these phrases is to practice reading in a way that sounds like the way they speak. Model how phrases should be read until the children read them with the proper intonation. As with word lists, phrase lists should be read with the teacher at least two times, with each child taking a turn reading a phrase aloud.

Level 43

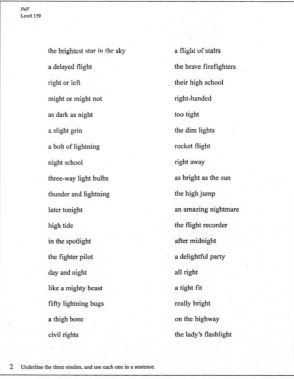

Level 159

Sentence Lists

Sentence lists provide an opportunity to teach children to pay attention to punctuation, such as stopping at periods or pausing at commas, which facilitates reading with expression. Sentence lists also provide practice in reading at an appropriate rate, neither too slowly nor too quickly.

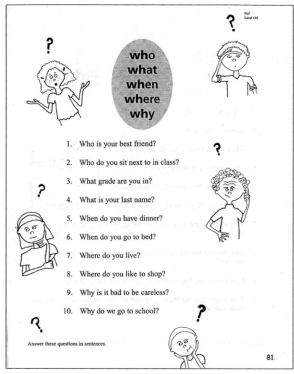

Level 135

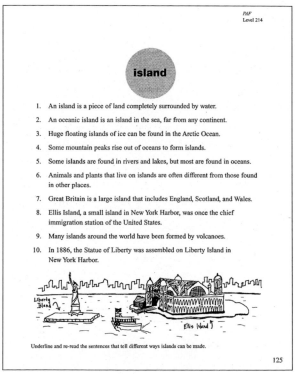

Level 214

Children should spend approximately fifteen minutes a day, more if needed, reading word, phrase, and sentence lists in their Stepping Up In Reading books with an adult. You should read the new list several times during the lesson and review previous lists if time allows. One technique for getting children to reread lists is to have them search for particular words or text. *(Can you find two things that are alive? Which phrase tells you where someone might be?)* You will find suggestions for these prompts on the bottom of each list. You can provide additional reading practice by sending the lists home to be read to an adult. Every list should be reread until it is read automatically, at the word recognition level.

Repeated readings develop word recognition and fluency, which are the basis for reading comprehension. The easier it is for children to read the text, the more they can focus on its meaning.

Readers

After you read with the children in their Stepping Up books, you will read aloud with them from the Merrill Readers. At this point in the lesson, the focus shifts from teaching phonics to teaching comprehension. This shift is possible because of the preparatory work that the children have done in their dictations and Stepping Up books. That work ensures that the children have enough word recognition and fluency to give their full attention to the meaning of the text. There is no need for further discussion about language structure. The ultimate goal of the instruction you do in the Merrill Readers is to give the students the skills they need to read with understanding, independent of a teacher's questioning and guidance.

Gather the children around a table or in a circle so that they can see each other and you while they read and discuss the book. Children will take turns reading aloud in random order while you stop them to offer corrections or elicit discussions.

In addition to helping children understand the text by asking questions about the content and discussing it, you need to teach them strategies to use when reading on their own. As children begin to monitor their own comprehension and apply reading strategies appropriately, they become independent learners.

Examples of some research-based strategies include:

Visualizing

Constructing mental images has been proven to be a helpful strategy for young children when they are reading fiction. Encourage children to *make a picture in their head* as they read. You can draw pictures on the board while reading with the children to show them how written words can be translated into images.

Predicting

Encourage students to make logical predictions as they read, and then have them stop periodically to verify whether they are right or wrong. Some chapter titles lend themselves to predictions (*Eggs for a Cake* might be about a bake sale, a party, or a cooking lesson); other titles do not *(Spelling, Bugs, and Plants)*. Examples of the types of predictions students may make while reading include how a character will solve a problem or what might happen next. Predictions do not have to be correct, but they must be logical.

Paraphrasing

Paraphrasing is an especially important reading strategy, because when readers put ideas into their own words, they understand and remember them better. Also, beginning readers have thousands more words in their spoken vocabularies than they are able to read. This is especially true when the children are using texts with highly controlled vocabularies – the discrepancy between what they can read and what they can say is vast.

You should encourage the children to discuss the text using their own words. *Can you think of another way to say that? What did Gus mean when he said Pam couldn't get a pet yet?* You particularly want to ask your students to paraphrase difficult sentences or concepts in the text. Similarly, you should be paraphrasing as you lead the discussions. When the text says, *Dan was mad,* ask, *Why was Dan so angry?* When the text says, *Kim has a bad cut on her leg,* ask, *How did she get injured?*

Remember, the reading vocabulary has to be controlled for beginning readers, but the language used to discuss the text can be varied and sophisticated.

• Retelling and Summarizing

Before you introduce the concept of summarizing, the children will need lots of practice re-telling stories, demonstrating that they remember details accurately and can put them in the proper order. Ask the children, *What happened?* at the end of the story.

Summarizing is a crucial but difficult skill that develops over years. To summarize, children must determine what is important and put that information into their own words. Over time, you should encourage the children to leave out unimportant or redundant details and focus on the main idea. Only after years of teacher modeling and feedback can children be expected to create summaries independently. The chapters in the novels that are read at the end of the Instructional Sequence provide excellent material for teaching and practicing summarizing.

When children do not understand the text, teach them to use one of these fix-up strategies:

• Rereading

Encourage children to go back to the text when they are confused, rather than having another child give the correct answer. When reading nonfiction, insist that children go back to the text to verify new information. *Where did the author say that?*

• Asking for help

Try to create an environment in which children feel comfortable asking questions about what they do not understand. Be sure to convey to your class that good readers always ask for help when they do not understand something.

When children make errors while reading aloud, their errors must be immediately corrected. Here are some common reading errors and examples of how to make corrections:

• If a child misreads a phonetic word, point to the misread word as a signal to the child to sound it out again.

• If a child misreads a red word, have him skywrite the word to trigger the correct response.

• If a child cannot read a word that contains a sound that has not been taught, say the word for the child. For example, supply the word *look* while children are learning short vowels.

- If a child skips words or loses his place, encourage him to run his finger in a continuous motion under the text *(finger gliding)*. Finger gliding can improve accuracy by helping the child focus his attention.

- If a child struggles with a word or reads a sentence word-by-word, have him reread the entire sentence. If the meaning of the sentence has been lost because of labored decoding, reread it for the group before calling on the next reader.

- If the meaning of a word is problematic, simply paraphrase or clarify the word quickly and continue with the story. When a child reads, *It is the dairy's job to kill the bacteria,* say: *So the dairy kills the bacteria—**the germs**—in the milk.*

Because all eight Merrill Readers have the same set of main characters and the same setting, a character chart is a useful graphic organizer. Displaying the chart will help the children learn the characters and their relationships. Beginning with the second Merrill Reader, Dig In, and continuing through the fourth reader, Get Set, you can add each major character to the chart as he or she is introduced. The character chart can be used before, during, or after the lesson, depending on the particular story and lesson goals.

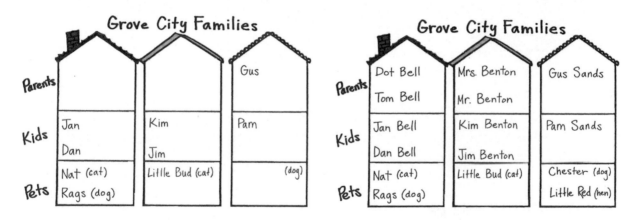

Character Chart at the end of Book B   Character Chart at the end of Book D

For some lessons, the reading material will come from the Merrill Skills Books that accompany each reader. These Skills Books should also be read with an adult for additional reading practice and not assigned as independent work.

The Skills Books offer you the opportunity to teach a range of language skills that are not taught in the readers, such as changing questions to statements, classification, synonyms, and antonyms. The Skills Books reinforce the vocabulary in the readers while providing different types of text, such as tables and graphs. Many of the pages can be done by having the children answer orally or circling the answers rather than writing them.

Repeated Readings

Rereading to an adult is an excellent strategy for improving accuracy, word recognition, and fluency. Therefore, the children should practice reading with someone at home every night. Each day you should send home lists from Stepping Up In Reading and stories from the Merrill Readers. For children without someone to read to at home or who need extra practice, be sure to provide more opportunities to read to an adult in school.

Once the children have graduated from the Merrills to chapter books, their reading homework should no longer involve rereading text. Rereading chapters disrupts the momentum of the story. Instead, have children read the next chapter or chapters independently for homework. You should review the chapters read at home in class the following day before reading the next chapter aloud with the children.

Reading to the Children

Set aside time each day to read aloud to the students from a variety of children's literature and nonfiction. Reading aloud is essential to help beginning readers develop comprehension, because it expands their background knowledge and exposes them to language that is more sophisticated than what they can read themselves. They hear vocabulary and grammar that they are not likely to hear in everyday speech. For children who are reading decodable text, reading aloud is also an opportunity to introduce them to a range of genres and text structures.

Reading to children allows them to experience reading not only as a skill to be mastered, but as an ongoing source of information and pleasure. This in turn motivates them to become independent readers. Try to read to your class everyday but remember that reading to children should never replace the critical time spent reading with them.

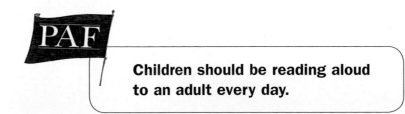

Children should be reading aloud to an adult every day.

Daily Lesson

Review
Introduction of New Material
Spelling Dictation
Reading
Reinforcement

Reinforcement

Each lesson concludes with activities for independent seat work or homework. What follows are some general suggestions for reinforcement activities that can be used at any point in the sequence.

Have the children reread a story in their Merrill Reader and complete one of the following activities:

- For Books A-C, illustrate the story.

- For Books D-H, answer one or two comprehension questions.

- For nonfiction selections in Books E-H, locate facts and write them in sentences.

Illustrating Stories

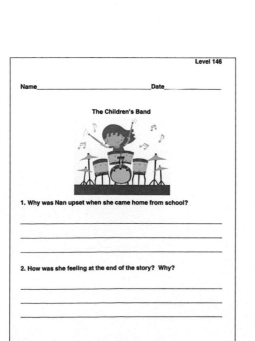

Answering Questions

Finding Facts

On days when your students have read pages in the Merrill Skills Books and done the activities orally, you may choose to have them answer the questions in writing as a reinforcement activity.

At every stage in the sequence, you should send home lists from Stepping Up for the children to read aloud to an adult. In addition, you can use Stepping Up to create assignments, such as having the children find words on the word lists that fit into certain categories, or asking them to use words from the lists in sentences.

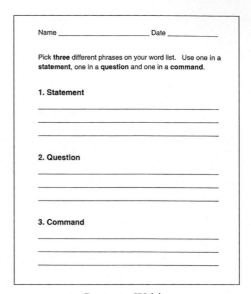

Categorizing   Sentence Writing

There are certain activities that should never be used for reinforcement. For example, never ask your students to write their spelling words multiple times, to do word searches, or to unscramble misspelled words. These activities have little to no instructional value, and they are especially inappropriate for children with learning issues.

While doing reinforcement activities at school or home, it is important for your students to spell words correctly even if that means asking for help from adults. Spelling words incorrectly reinforces errors. If a child asks for help spelling a word, either ask him to sound out the word (if it is composed of sounds he knows) or tell him how to spell it. It is better that you or a parent spells words for the child than for him to practice writing them incorrectly.

Sample Lesson Sequence

Here is how the daily lesson would look for the introduction of the sound /ĕ/

1. Review Do a review of previously taught sounds, red words, and suffixes using the review pack.

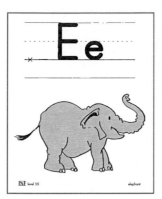

2. Introduction of New Material Then teach the sound using the keyword from the Alphabet Picture Cards.

You also teach the motor pattern for writing the letter using the Handwriting Program for Print.

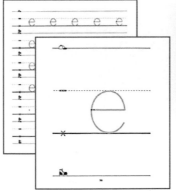

3. Spelling Dictation Give a dictation with the new sound, using words and a sentence you have selected from the Teacher Handbook.

4. Reading Now read with the children. First you will read words and phrases with the new sound in Stepping Up In Reading to practice decoding, word recognition, and reading fluency.

Then read stories with the new sound in the Merrill Reader for additional reading practice and to teach comprehension strategies.

Look at the Pets

Jan and Kim took little Pam
to look at pets.
Pam looks at cats and pups.

Pam ran to her dad.
"Can I get a pet?" she said.

Gus said, "You have a pup!"

"Can I get a cat?" said Pam.

"Not yet," said Gus.
"I cannot let you have a cat
and a pup."

Little Pam is sad.

5. Reinforcement As a final reinforcement activity, you might ask the children to reread the story independently and illustrate it.

INSTRUCTIONAL SEQUENCE

This section of the handbook contains directions for using the instructional sequence, ideas for lesson planning, an overview of what is taught in PAF, and the full instructional sequence.

PAF must be taught in a step-by-step progression, with students learning each step before progressing to the next. Every level in the sequence builds on the skills and concepts taught in previous levels. When properly implemented, the program should take approximately three years to complete, although the exact length of time will depend on your students' abilities and the amount of time allocated for reading instruction. In general, each level in this program will require more than one day of instruction to complete. There is no set formula, however, for how long to spend at a given level. Some levels take longer than others, particularly when the material is complex. On most days you will find that there is no new material to introduce and the lesson will focus on review, practice, and reinforcement of prior material.

Every level in the instructional sequence lists the skills and concepts to be taught, materials to be used, words and sentences to be used for spelling dictations, and specific teaching instructions.

The words on each list have been controlled to contain only the sounds children have already learned. The sentences are composed of words the children can sound out and of previously taught red words. Keep in mind that you do not have to dictate every word and sentence listed at a given level. Only dictate as many as necessary to teach the skill.

On the next page you will find one example of a level in the sequence.

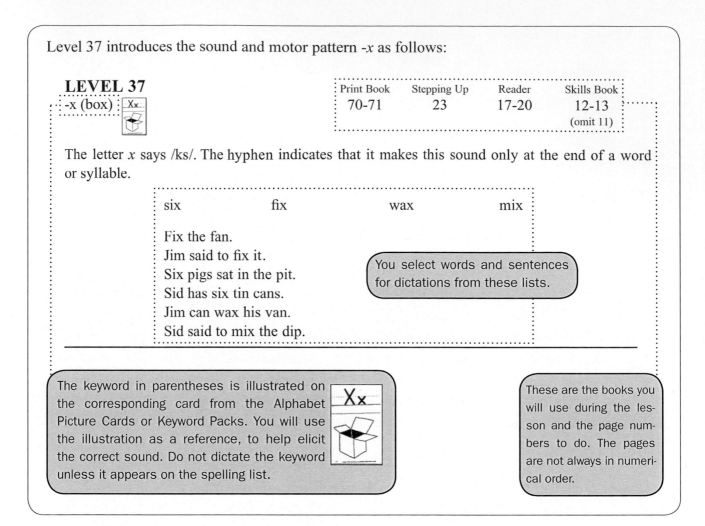

Level 37 introduces the sound and motor pattern -*x* as follows:

LEVEL 37

-x (box) Xx

Print Book	Stepping Up	Reader	Skills Book
70-71	23	17-20	12-13
			(omit 11)

The letter *x* says /ks/. The hyphen indicates that it makes this sound only at the end of a word or syllable.

six   fix   wax   mix

Fix the fan.
Jim said to fix it.
Six pigs sat in the pit.
Sid has six tin cans.
Jim can wax his van.
Sid said to mix the dip.

You select words and sentences for dictations from these lists.

The keyword in parentheses is illustrated on the corresponding card from the Alphabet Picture Cards or Keyword Packs. You will use the illustration as a reference, to help elicit the correct sound. Do not dictate the keyword unless it appears on the spelling list.

These are the books you will use during the lesson and the page numbers to do. The pages are not always in numerical order.

As you proceed through the curriculum, you will find levels marked for reading only. The concepts presented for reading only are to be practiced using the Stepping Up in Reading books and Merrill Readers but are not included in dictations.

Keep in mind that while there are no new words for dictation at a for reading only level, some teachers use the opportunity to give a review dictation of previously misspelled words. It is up to you, based on the specific needs of your students, whether to give a review dictation at this level or to skip it to focus only on the reading.

Finally, the instructional sequence will tell you when to stop to give proficiency tests. Remember, the success of this program depends on completing the sequence in order without omissions. This includes administering the proficiency tests when indicated. Your students' performance on the proficiency tests will help you determine when they need more opportunities for review and when you can proceed to a new level.

Getting Started

In order to begin the sequence, children must be able to isolate the initial sound in a word (*What is the first sound in* apple?). This is a basic phonemic awareness task. While there are other, more difficult phonemic awareness tasks, such as blending sounds into words for reading (*b-a-t: bat*) and segmenting words into sounds for spelling (*bat: b-a-t*), these skills will be taught throughout the program and are not prerequisites to getting started.

If you are using PAF as a preventive program in kindergarten or first grade, you should begin at Level 1. Although some of your students may demonstrate isolated skills, such as knowing the sounds of letters or writing letters correctly, they all must be taught to associate each letter with its sound **and** motor pattern, so you should start the entire group at Level 1. By Level 3, the children will begin to spell and read words.

If you are using PAF as a remedial program, you should download the PAF Placement Test to determine at which level to begin. For older students who are still learning the alphabet, display the Cursive Alphabet Picture Cards rather than the Alphabet Picture Cards, because they are more sophisticated.

Planning the Lesson

There are two parts to planning a lesson: (1) filling out a lesson plan form, including the words and sentences for spelling dictation and pages to be used in the materials; and (2) writing directly in your copy of the Merrill Readers to plan the comprehension part of your lesson. While you are teaching, be sure to make notes about student errors to help you plan future lessons. The effectiveness of your instruction depends on careful lesson planning and monitoring the students' daily performance.

In the Appendix, you will find three sample lessons that demonstrate how to fill out the lesson plan form and how to create the comprehension lesson in the Merrill Readers. These sample lessons include stories in a variety of genres, from a simple decodable story, to a retelling of a fable, to a nonfiction selection. When it comes to reading comprehension, there are many effective ways to introduce, discuss, and review a story. The sample lessons provided represent only a few of the many possible approaches.

Before reading further, take time to review the three sample lesson plans in the Appendix. These will give you an idea of what your lesson plans should encompass.

Part I: Filling Out the Lesson Plan Form

In addition to the sample lessons, the Appendix contains four blank lesson plan forms. Three of the forms are for general use, and which one you choose depends on the level you are teaching. The fourth form is designed specifically for teaching red words.

• First, choose six to nine root words that you want to dictate from the list of words provided in this handbook. You should dictate fewer words to young students who are just learning to form the letters.

• Once your students have learned suffixes, begin adding them to some of the words used for dictation. For example, when teaching *ai,* the word *rain* is listed, but you may decide to also dictate the words *raining* and *rained.* Be careful not to add suffixes that require the application of a spelling rule that the students have not yet learned (*run* + *ing* = *running*).

• Next, choose one to three sentences for dictation, making sure to choose some sentences that contain words you will plan to first dictate in isolation.

• Finally, decide how many days you plan to allot to teaching this level and how you will allocate the three different reading materials: Stepping Up In Reading books, Merrill Readers, and Merrill Skills Books. Be sure to organize your lessons so that you read and reread the lists in Stepping Up with your children *every day.* As for Merrill Readers and Skills Books, decide whether to use one or the other, or a combination of both, on any given day. Write the page numbers to be read on your lesson plan form.

Part II: Planning for Oral Reading in the Merrill Readers

• Read the selection for the day and decide what the story is about. For fiction, ask yourself: *What happened in the story? How did the characters feel or change? Is there a main idea? Is there a moral?* For nonfiction: *What are the important facts to learn?*

• Next, make notes about places in the text where comprehension is likely to break down because of unfamiliar vocabulary or grammar. (This is an area of particular difficulty for students with oral language problems and for students learning English.) Recognizing potential trouble spots in the story will help you plan ahead for where to stop for questions and discussion.

• Finally, decide what you will do with your class before, during and after reading a story. Write these plans directly in your copy of the Merrill Readers. Remember, every reading comprehension lesson must be done in a group format, with you, the teacher, leading the students in oral reading and group discussion.

Before Reading

Decide how to introduce the story to the group. Think of ways to give the students a purpose for the reading, such as:

- Using the title to make a prediction. *(The title of today's story is "Look at the Pets." What do you think the setting of the story might be? Let's read and see if you are right.)*

- Connecting the story to a previous selection. *(Yesterday we read that Jim decided to save his money for a fishing trip with his grandpa. Today we will find out if he was successful.)*

- Creating interest. *(Today we are going to read another story about that mischievous cat, Nat. Wait until you see the trouble he gets into!)*

Usually, with the everyday language of beginning readers, it is not necessary to teach new vocabulary prior to reading the story. The vocabulary is best taught while reading the story aloud as a class, because the words will make more sense in context. Also, Merrill stories tend to be about everyday activities that require little background knowledge to understand. For most of the stories in the readers, the best prereading activities will be those that set a purpose for reading.

During Reading

Deciding in advance where to stop for questions and discussions is a critical part of lesson planning. Plan to stop at logical breaks in the story to discuss what is happening and how the characters are responding. Be sure to ask questions that keep students focused on the main ideas of the story, *not* on unimportant details. Be careful not to ask too many questions, as this can disrupt the flow of the story and impede comprehension. On the other hand, if you ask too few questions, you may not notice when comprehension has broken down. In general, you should plan to ask more questions when reading nonfiction texts than fiction, because these texts will contain new information for the children to learn.

When preparing your lessons, keep in mind that the quality of the questions is as important as the quantity. Good questions focus students on significant information in the text and stimulate thoughtful responses and class discussions. *(What does Grandma mean when she said that Dan has a heart of gold?)* Avoid asking literal questions or questions that elicit simple yes or no responses. *(Was there a new girl in Jane's class?)*

When reading fiction, remember that your students' comprehension depends on their ability to understand the characters' feelings and motivations. In other words, you want your students to be able to put themselves in someone else's shoes. It is not important for children to imagine or guess how *they* would feel under the same circumstances. It is very important for them to empathize with the characters. For this reason, you should avoid asking questions that thrust the reader into the story and discourage empathy for the characters, as this will impede deep understanding of the story.

> Ask: *How do you think Mike is feeling since he wasn't invited to the party?*
> Avoid: *How would you feel if your friend didn't invite you to a party?*

> Ask: *What do you think will happen now that Josh told everyone Amy's secret?*
> Avoid: *Have you ever told a secret that someone had asked you to keep?*

After Reading

Plan a discussion that encourages your students to think about what they have just read and helps them organize and reinforce the important ideas. Be sure the discussion relates to the central events and characters of the story or, with nonfiction, to the relevant information presented. Discussions that focus only on the students' personal experiences or feelings can interfere with their understanding of the story.

> Ask: *What did Peter learn about how to be a good friend?*
> Avoid: *Who is your best friend? Why do you like him?*
>
> Ask*: What did we learn about how snakes protect themselves?*
> Avoid*: Do you like snakes? Why?*
>
> Ask: *What made Gail's birthday party so special for her?*
> Avoid: *What was the most special birthday party you ever had?*

Some effective ways to promote concluding discussions include having young students retell the story in sequence and, with older students, helping them generate a summary of the text.

Instructional Sequence

The instructional sequence consists of 215 levels, divided into nine sections. The first section covers the concepts that your students must master in order to begin reading the first reader. Each of the next eight sections corresponds to a different reader.

On the following two pages, you will find an overview of the sequence. For a detailed list of the contents, see the Instructional Sequence at-a-Glance in the Appendix.

CURRICULUM OVERVIEW

The Curriculum Overview is a summary of when skills are taught in the sequence. The summary does not, however, list reading comprehension strategies, because they are taught throughout the sequence rather than at any one particular level. These include: visualizing, predicting, paraphrasing, summarizing, and rereading. Beginning with Book G, underlining and note-taking are introduced as well. Language concepts—for example, multiple-meaning words, idioms, pronoun referents, and categorization—also spiral through the sequence. Finally, whenever possible, the children are made aware of text structures, such as: problem and solution, sequence of events, list of facts, cause and effect, and compare and contrast.

LEVELS	**Levels 1-74** *Book A (I Can)* *Book B (Dig In)* *Book C (Catch On)*	**Levels 75-129** *Book D (Get Set)* *Book E (Step Up)*
PHONOGRAMS	alphabet short vowels ch, sh, th -ve -y = /ī/ open syllable words	initial and final blends -ng, -nk triple blends ar, or -all -ll, -ss, -ff
RED WORDS	the of from to are were you they very your put do said was goes	don't one off won't none walk who done talk school there where want some friend what come full

SYLLABICATION		open syllables
		closed syllables
		r-controlled syllables
		syllable division:
		  VCCV
		  VCV

MISCELLANEOUS CONCEPTS	capitalization final punctuation word families multiple meaning words plural s possessive s -s (verb form) compound words abbreviations root words suffixes: -ing, -ed	contractions synonyms antonyms suffixes: -ed, -er, -est, -es, -ful, -less

CURRICULUM OVERVIEW *(continued)*

LEVELS	Levels 130-158 *Book F (Lift Off)*	Levels 159-186 *Book G (Take Flight)*	Levels 187-215 *Book H* *(Break Through)* Chapter Books
PHONOGRAMS	silent e vowels long vowel teams igh wh- -y = /ē/ a = /ū/	-en -et -ore soft c soft g -age wr, kn eigh twin consonants -ild, -ind -old, -ost, old er, ir, ur, ou, ow = /ou/ al = /all/ w(or) = /wer/ w(ar) = /wor	-rr o = /ŭ/ ea = /ĕ/ ea = /ā/ ear = /er/ au, aw silent b, h, and t oo = /o͞o/, /o͝o/ -ew = /ū/, /o͞o/ ou, ui , ue = /o͞o/ ie = /ē/, /ī/ oi, oy aught, ought gu- ph
RED WORDS	could been would does should pretty their only sure again because against says	woman built women any once many laugh together people water build	father tough buy enough half ocean rough island Wednesday
SPELLING RULES	silent e rule -ck	doubling rule -dge	y rule adding s to y words

SYLLABICATION	silent e syllables
	vowel team syllables
		syllable division:
		  VCCCV
		special syllable
		  endings
		multisyllable root
		  words
			-tion
			-sion
			-ture
			-ain

MISCELLANEOUS CONCEPTS	nouns verbs adjectives adverbs homonyms suffixes: -y, -ly		

The sequence begins with teaching the sounds of the alphabet and how to read and spell words made of these sounds. You can download an image of the Alphabet Picture Cards to send home to parents as a reference for the correct sounds.

DOWNLOAD
PAFprogram.com

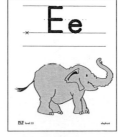

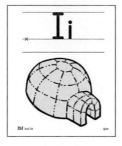

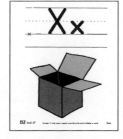

Levels 1-16

Handwriting Program for Print
First Steps In Reading
Alphabet Picture Cards
Pocket Chart Alphabet
Review Pack I

Preparation for Book A

LEVEL 1			Print Book	First Steps
c (cat)			1-3	1-3

All sounds are introduced with the lowercase form of the letter. The letter c will be the first card in the phonogram section of your review pack.

LEVEL 2			Print Book	First Steps
a (apple)			4-5	4-6

With the introduction of /ă/, begin to use the terms *vowel* and *consonant*. Tell children that some of the letters are very special, that these letters are called vowels, and that every word must have at least one vowel. The vowels in Review Pack I and in the Pocket Chart Alphabet Cards are printed on colored cards to help distinguish them from consonants.

LEVEL 3			Print Book	First Steps
t (tiger)			6-7	7-10

Begin spelling dictations and introduce the pocket chart with the letters *c*, *a*, and *t*.

at	cat

LEVEL 4			Print Book	First Steps
d (dog)			8-9	11-15

dad

LEVEL 5			Print Book	First Steps
g (girl)			10-11	16-19

You will teach the concept of multiple meaning words using page 19 in First Steps In Reading.

tag	gag

LEVEL 6			Print Book	First Steps
s (sun)			12-13	20-24

sat	sad	gas	sag

LEVEL 7
f (fish)

	Print Book	First Steps
	14-17	25-29

fat   fad

LEVEL 8
m (moon)

	Print Book	First Steps
	18-19	30-36

Teach the children to count the number of times they hit the writing line as they write.

1   2   3

am   mad   mat

LEVEL 9
l (lion)

	Print Book	First Steps
	20-21	37-40

lad   gal

LEVEL 10
Red Word: *a*
Capital A
Use of capitals and periods

	Print Book	First Steps
	22-23	41-44

This is the first red word. It is a little tricky, because the children have just learned to associate the sound /ă/ with the letter *a* at Level 2. Now you are going to tell them that when the letter *a* stands by itself, it says /ŭ/. To avoid confusion, you will dictate the word in phrases and sentences, not in isolation. Also, there is no card for this word in Review Pack I. The red word has to be taught at this time, because it appears in the reader.

a lad   a dad
a gal   a tag
a mat   a fat cat

A cat sat.
A dad sat.
A gal sat.
A fat cat sat.

LEVEL 11
h (hammer)

	Print Book	First Steps
	24-25	45-48

had   hat   ham

A cat had a ham.
A lad had a hat.

LEVEL 12
p (pumpkin)

			Print Book	First Steps
			26-27	49-54

tap	map	pad	cap
lap	pal	pat	

A dad had a map.
A gal had a cap.

LEVEL 13
n (nest)

	Print Book	First Steps
	28-29	55-61

Teach the children to count the number of times they hit the writing line as they write.

Teach the word *and* even though it contains a consonant blend, because it is a common word that increases the complexity of the dictated sentences.

can	man	tan	nap
and	pan	fan	

A sad man sat.
A man can pat a cat.
A man had a gas can.
A fat cat had a nap.
A man had a ham and a pan.
A cat had a pan and a mat.

LEVEL 14
Red Word: *I*

	Print Book	First Steps
	30-31	62-63

The word *I* is another tricky red word, because it is phonetic. It is only taught as a red word, because it is always capitalized. Like the red word *a*, the word *I* has no card in Review Pack I and is not practiced in isolation.

I had a nap.
I am a man.
I had a tan hat.
I am a fat cat.
I can pat a cat.
I had a pan and a ham.

LEVEL 15
Plural s

	Print Book	First Steps
	32-33	64

This is the first suffix taught. At this level, it is only added to words when it makes the sound /s/, not /z/. Tell the children that sometimes when you want to show that you have more than one of something, you add the letter *s*. Begin the suffix section of your review pack by adding the *-s* card. You will do the review by asking children, *Which letter shows more than one?*

Here's what you should do:
• Ask the children to write *cat,* and use it in a sentence for them: *My friend has a cat.*
• Tell them to make the word say *cats*: *I have two cats.*
• Ask them to add the letter *s* to the words they have already written.

cats   hats   maps   caps

I had tan hats.
A man had maps.
A dad had cats.
I had hats and caps.

If the children have difficulty reading words with a plural *s* have them
• cover the final *s* with one finger,
• read the word without the plural *s*, then
• uncover the *s* and read the whole word.

LEVEL 16
Capital N

	Print Book	First Steps
	34-35	65-68

Teach the use of capitals for names.

I am Nat.
I am fat Nat.
I can pat Nat.
I am mad at Nat.
A man can pat Nat.

> **Levels 17-33**
>
> Handwriting Program for Print
> Stepping Up In Reading 1
> Merrill Reader – Book A
> Merrill Skills Book A
> Alphabet Picture Cards
> Pocket Chart Alphabet
> Review Pack I

Merrill Book A - *I Can*

LEVEL 17
Red Word: *is*

	Print Book	Stepping Up	Reader	Skills Book
	36-37	1	5-6*	2-3* (omit 1)

A few common phonetic words needed by beginning readers (such as *is* and *you*) are included as red words until their phonetic elements are taught later in the sequence. This is the first word in the red word section of your review pack.

In order for the children to write *is*, they must be taught the motor pattern using the letter name *i*, not the sound /ĭ/.

Nat is a cat.
Nat is fat.
Nat is a fat cat.
Nat is sad.
Nat is a sad cat.

LEVEL 18
Red Word: *the*
Question Marks (for reading only)

	Print Book	Stepping Up	Reader	Skills Book
	38-39	2	7-8	4-5

In order for the children to write *the*, they must be taught the motor patterns for *e* using the letter name, not the sound. Begin a Red Word Chart, adding each word as it is taught throughout the year.

the fan   the fat cat
the maps   the tan hat
the caps   the gas can

I had the caps.
I am mad at the man.
Nat had the ham.
A man pats the cats.
A man had the maps.
A man can pat the cat.

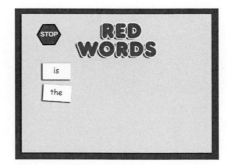

*If you are using the 2016 version of the Merrill Reasers and Skills Books, the page numbers may be off by one page.

The red words listed in this sequence are taught for reading and spelling, and are practiced in dictations and on sentence lists. There are other sight words in the readers (circled before each story) that are not drilled for mastery, because they are taught as phonetic words at a subsequent level. For example, on page 9, children will encounter the circled word *on*. Tell them the word in the circle before reading the story, and supply it if needed while they read.

The reader introduces question marks. Make sure the children attend to the final punctuation and read the questions with proper intonation.

LEVEL 19	Print Book	Stepping Up	Reader	Skills Book
Capital T	40-41	3	9-10	6-7

The cat is fat.
The man had the hats.
The fan is tan.
The cats can nap.
The man had a gas can.
The man is mad at Nat.

LEVEL 20	Print Book	Stepping Up	Reader	Skills Book
Capital D	42-43	4	11-12	8-9

Dad is a man.
Dan had the maps.
Dad is mad at Dan.
Dad and Dan nap.
Dad and Dan had the caps.
Dad and Dan pat the cats.

LEVEL 21	Print Book	Stepping Up	Reader	Skills Book
j (jet)	44-45	5	13-16	10-16

Exclamation Marks (for reading only)

The reader introduces exclamations. Make sure the children attend to the final punctuation and read the exclamations with proper intonation.

jam

Dan and I had the jam.
The cat had the jam.
Dad had ham and jam.
I had the jam.
The man had the jam.

LEVEL 22

b (boy)

	Print Book	Stepping Up	Reader	Skills Book
	46-47	6	17-20	17-21

With the introduction of the letter *b*, confusion may arise between *b* and *d*. These letters sound and look alike. One way to help children discriminate these letters is to emphasize the difference in how the letters are written. The *b* is a **tall** letter and goes **away** from the green line. The *d* is a **two o'clock** letter and goes **to** the green line.

 Download the *b* and *d* chart and cut it in half. Place the *b* on the left side of the board and the *d* on the right side. These images can be reduced and placed on individual desks if needed.

bat   bag   tab   jab

Dan is at bat.
The bag is tan.
Dad can bat.
Dad had a tan bag.
The can had a tab.
The man had the bats.

In a follow-up lesson, ask children to spell the word *bad*.
Dictate the following sentences:

Dad had a bad can.
A jab is bad.
The ham is bad.

LEVEL 23

r (robot)

	Print Book	Stepping Up	Reader	Skills Book
	48-49	7	21-23	23-25 (omit 22)

ran   rat   rag

Dad and Dan ran.
Dan had a rag.
The man ran and ran.
The cat ran at the rats.
The rat had a nap.
The bad rat had the ham.

LEVEL 24
Red Word: *to*

	Print Book	Stepping Up	Reader	Skills Book
	50-51	8	24-26	26-27

In order for children to write *to,* they must be taught the motor pattern for *o,* although the sound /ŏ/ is not taught yet.

Nat ran to Dan.
I had to nap.
The rat ran to the mat.
Dan had to bat.
Dad ran to the man.
Dan had to pat the sad cat.

LEVEL 25
v (valentine)

	Print Book	Stepping Up	Reader	Skills Book
	52-53	9	27-30	29-31
				(omit 28)

van

The man had a van.
The van is tan.
Dad had a tan van.
Dan ran to the van.
The man ran the van.
The man and I ran to the van.

LEVEL 26
s as in *tags*
Capital J

	Print Book	Stepping Up	Reader	Skills Book
	54-55	10	31-32	32-36

Plural *s* sometimes makes the sound /z/. Point out the new sound without reference to the letter *z*. The words *as* and *has* have been included, although they are not plurals, because they are common.

as	has		
cans	hams	bags	rags
vans	pans	fans	tags

Jan has to bat.
Jan has the bags.
I am as mad as Jan.
Dan and Jan had the rags.
Jan ran to the vans.
Jan has the hams and the jam.

LEVEL 27
Possessive s

	Stepping Up	Reader	Skills Book
	11	33-38	37-40

Jan's cat	Jan's bag
Dan's hat	the cat's mat
Nat's pan	the man's van

Dan has Jan's bag.

Jan has Nat's mat.

The cat's mat is tan.

The rat ran to the cat's pan.

Dan ran to the man's van.

Nat is Dan and Jan's cat.

LEVEL 28	Print Book	Stepping Up	Reader	Skills Book
y- (yarn)	56-57	12	39-44	41-47
				(omit 48)

The letter *y* only makes its consonant sound when it is the first letter of a word or syllable.

yam

Dan had a yam.

Nat has Jan's yam.

Dad has the yams.

Jan's yam is fat.

Jan has hams and yams.

The rat ran to the yam.

LEVEL 29	Print Book	Stepping Up	Reader	Skills Book
Red Words: *you, your*	58-59	13-14	45-50	49-52

In order for children to write *you,* they must be taught the motor pattern for *u.* The sound /ŭ/, however, is not taught yet.

The cat ran to you.

Jan's cat ran to you.

Dan can tag you.

I am mad at you.

Jan and you can pat Nat.

Dan and you had the bats.

Nat is your cat.

Dad ran your van.

Jan is your pal.

Jan has your bags.

I can pat your cat.

Dan has your bat.

LEVEL 30	Print Book	Stepping Up	Reader	Skills Book
Capital Y	60-61	15	51-56	53-59

You had a nap.

You and Jan ran.

You can pat your cat.

You ran to the van.

You had Dan's rag.

Your cat is Nat.

Your dad's van is tan.

Your cat has a yam.

Your bag has a tag.

Your dad had a nap.

LEVEL 31	Print Book	Stepping Up	Reader	Skills Book
Capital S	62-63	16	57-62	60-66

> Sam is a man.
> Sam's van is tan.
> Sam has your bag.
> Sam is mad at you.
> Jan has Sam's map.

LEVEL 32	Print Book	Stepping Up	Reader	Skills Book
Capital R	64-65	17	63-68	68-72 (omit 67)

The word *wag* appears in the Reader and Skills Book and must be read for the children until they learn *w* = /w/ (Level 35).

> Rags and Nat ran.
> You can pat Rags.
> Rags ran to the van.
> Rags has your cap.
> Nat ran to Rags.

LEVEL 33	Print Book	Stepping Up	Reader	Skills Book
-s (verb form)	66-67	18	69-77	73-80
Capital F				

The goal is to make the children aware that final *s* not only forms plurals (Level 15) but also describes action. *(The cat naps on the mat.)* The children are not expected to distinguish nouns and verbs but should be aware that final *s* has several meanings.

> naps   bats   taps   pats

> Sam naps.
> Rags naps.
> Fat Nat pats the bag.
> Sam pats Rags.
> Fat Nat bats at Rags.
> Fat Nat taps the pan.

**Time to read the instructions on pages 149-153,
and give Proficiency Test #1.**

> **Levels 34-52**
>
> Handwriting Program for Print
> Stepping Up In Reading 1
> Merrill Reader – Book B
> Merrill Skills Book B
> Alphabet Picture Cards
> Pocket Chart Alphabet
> Review Pack I

Merrill Book B - *Dig In*

LEVEL 34	Stepping Up	Reader	Skills Book
i (igloo)	19-20	5-10*	2-5*
			(omit 1)

The contraction *it's* appears in the reader. Simply explain to the children that *it's* stands for the words *it* and *is*. The concept of contractions is not introduced until Level 76.

Remove *is* from your review pack and the Red Word Chart.

if	big	dig	lip
in	hit	fit	tin
it	him	hid	pit
is	sit	pin	bit
did	his	pig	rip

Dan hid the pin.
Sam sits in his van.
The map has a big rip.
Dad digs a big pit.
Rags is as big as a pig.
The pigs fit in the van.

You will find a sample lesson for this level on pages 200 and 201.

After working with the new vowel for two or three lessons, do a divided dictation in which children have to distinguish between the two vowels they have learned, ă and ĭ. Have them fold their papers in half and write an *a* at the top of one column and an *i* at the top of the second column. Tell the children to listen for the vowel sound and decide in which column to write each word. Dictate the following words in this order: dad, bag, it, at, big, did.

a	**i**

---

*If you are using the 2016 version of the Merrill Reasers and Skills Books, the page numbers may be off by one page.

LEVEL 35	Print Book	Stepping Up	Reader	Skills Book
w (web)	68-69	21	11-13	6-7

The compound word *into* appears in the reader. Simply explain to the children that the word is made up of two smaller words. The concept of compound words is not introduced until Level 66.

wag   win   wig

Rags can wag.
Jan has a wig.
Jim can win.
Rags wags at Sam.
Jim bats and wins.
Jan has hats and wigs.

LEVEL 36		Stepping Up	Reader	Skills Book
Red Word: *said*		22	14-16	8-10

Although you are using the word *said*, be sure that any additional sentences created for dictation do not require quotation marks.

Dad said to sit in his van.
Jim said his pig digs.
Dan said Jim is big.
Dad said Jim can bat and win.
I said I am mad at Rags.
Jim said his bag has a rip in it.

LEVEL 37	Print Book	Stepping Up	Reader	Skills Book
-x (box)	70-71	23	17-20	12-13
				(omit 11)

The letter *x* says /ks/ at the end of a word or syllable.

six   fix   wax   mix

Fix the fan.
Jim said to fix it.
Six pigs sat in the pit.
Sid has six tin cans.
Jim can wax his van.
Sid said to mix the dip.

LEVEL 38

Use of Question Marks

	Stepping Up	Reader	Skills Book
	24	21-22	14-16

Before dictating, provide large and small models of a question mark to trace and copy.

> Is his pig big?
> Did Sid fix the ax?
> Is his pin in the bag?
> Did Jim wax Sid's van?
> Is Nat Jim's cat?
> Did the six pigs fit in the van?

LEVEL 39

Red Word: *of*

	Stepping Up	Reader	Skills Book
	25	23-25	17-19

> Six of the pigs ran to Jim.
> Is the can of gas in the van?
> Rags had bits of ham.
> Jan had a bag of yams.
> Did Sam mix the can of wax?
> Jim hid six of the bags.

LEVEL 40

Capital C

	Print Book	Stepping Up	Reader	Skills Book
	72-73	26	26-28	20-21

> Cats and pigs can nap.
> Can you mix the can of wax?
> Cats can sit in vans.
> Can Jim fix the rip in his cap?
> Can you dig a pit and sit in it?
> Can six of the pigs fit into your van?

LEVEL 41

k (king)

	Print Book	Stepping Up	Reader	Skills Book
	74-75	27	29-34	23-26
				(omit 22)

The usual spellings of /k/ are *c* at the beginning of a word and *k* at the end. At this level, the children do not know when to use *c* at the beginning of a word and when to use *k,* and must be told directly. *(Spell* kid. *Use a* k.*)*

Begin to use a character chart as described on page 29 in this handbook.

> kid   kit
>
> Dad has his kit.
> Six kids can fit in the van.
> Is Jim a big kid?
> Did the kids win?
> Is it Jim's kit?

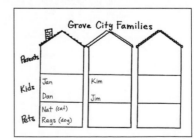

| **LEVEL 42** | | Print Book | Stepping Up | Reader | Skills Book |
| z (zebra) | | 76-77 | 28 | 35-38 | 27-32 |

zip   zigzag

Jim zips his bag.
The rip is a zigzag.
The kids ran in a zigzag.
Can you zip it?
Jan ran zigzag.
Did Sam zip the bag?

LEVEL 43		Print Book	Stepping Up	Reader	Skills Book
Capital P		78-79	29-30	39-42	33-36
					(omit 37)

Pat Jim's cat.
Pigs can nap.
Pam is a kid.
Pat the cat in your lap.
Pam's kit is in your van.
Pigs can sit in a pit.

LEVEL 44			Stepping Up	Reader	Skills Book
u (umbrella)			31-32	43-46	39-42
					(omit 38)

up	bus	cut	tub
us	mud	rug	cub
run	sun	tug	gum
but	bug	nut	hug
fun	cup	rub	dug

It is fun to run in the sun.
Rags runs to us.
Pam has nuts and gum.
Can Pam zip it up?
Is Sid's van as big as a bus?
Did the bugs run to the cup?

After working with the new vowel for two or three lessons, do a divided dictation in which children have to distinguish between the three vowels they have learned, ă, ĭ, and ŭ. Prefold their paper into thirds. Have them write one vowel at the top of each column. Tell children to listen for the vowel sound and decide in which column to write each word. Dictate these words: big, fan, but, bug, pin, fun, hat, bag, hit.

a	i	u

LEVEL 45	Print Book	Stepping Up	Reader	Skills Book
Capital B	80-81	33	47-48	43-45

Bud is Jim's cat.
Bud runs and runs.
Bugs can sit in the mud.
Did Bud run to the bus?
Can Bud run in a zigzag?
Did Bud sit in the sun?

LEVEL 46	Print Book	Stepping Up	Reader	Skills Book
-ve as in *give*	82-83	34-35	49-54	46-48
Capital G				

No word in the English language ends with the letter *v*. A silent *e* is added, which does not change the vowel sound.

have   give   live

Give the cup of nuts to Gus.
Give Gus a hug.
The pigs live in a hut.
Did Gus have fun?
Is Gus Pam's dad?
Did the kids give up?

LEVEL 47	Print Book	Stepping Up	Reader	Skills Book
qu (queen)	84-85	36	55-58	49-53

quit   quiz

Did you have a quiz?
Did you give Jim his quiz?
Dad said to quit it.
Pam had a big quiz.
Did the kid quit?
I said to quit it.

LEVEL 48	Print Book	Stepping Up	Reader	Skills Book
Red Word: *are*	86-87	37	59-62	55-58 (omit 54)

The cubs are in the mud.
Pups are fun.
Pam and Gus are in the bus.
Are you up?
Are the mugs yours?
Are Gus and Pam in the bus?

LEVEL 49	Print Book	Stepping Up	Reader	Skills Book
Capital K	88-89	38	63-66	59-63

Kim's cat is Bud.
Kim and Jim are kids.
Kids can have fun in the mud.
Can Kim give Jan a hug?
Are Kim and Pam pals?
Did Kim have a quiz?

LEVEL 50		Stepping Up	Reader	Skills Book
Red Word: *they*		39	67-70	65-68
				(omit 64)

They are Kim's pals.
They had to give Jim his bat.
They can run and have fun.
Can they hum?
Did they give up?
Are they your cups?

LEVEL 51	Print Book	Stepping Up	Reader	Skills Book
Capital H	90-91	40	71-74	69-73

His pup is in the tub.
Hats and bats are in the bus.
Ham and nuts are in the pan.
Has Gus cut his lip?
Have they had fun?
Have they dug a pit?

LEVEL 52	Print Book	Stepping Up	Reader	Skills Book
Capital M	92-93	41	75-77	74-79
Red Word: *put*				

Mix it up.
Max put nuts in the cup.
Max puts the maps in the bus.
Did Max put bugs in the can?
Max said to put nuts in the mix.
Did Max put the jam in his bag?

Time to stop teaching and give Proficiency Test #2.

> **Levels 53-74**
>
> Handwriting Program for Print
> Stepping Up In Reading 1
> Merrill Reader – Book C
> Merrill Skills Book C
> Alphabet Picture Cards
> Pocket Chart Alphabet
> Keyword Picture Cards
> Review Pack I

Merrill Book C - *Catch On*

LEVEL 53
o (octopus)

		Stepping Up	Reader	Skills Book
		42-45	5-8*	1-4*

on	lot	fox	hop
not	dog	mom	job
box	pot	top	jog
got	hot	mop	log

Tom got a lot of hot dogs.
Mom put hot suds in the pot.
Dot is Jan's mom.
Did Tom quit his job?
Can a fox live in a log?
Did the bug hop on top of the box?

After working with the new vowel for two or three lessons, do a divided dictation in which children have to distinguish between the vowels *u* and *o*. Have the children fold their papers in half and write one vowel at the top of each column. Tell children to listen for the vowel sound and decide in which column to write each word. Dictate these words: hot, nut, dug, not, top, cut, hop, pot, rub, hug.

u	o

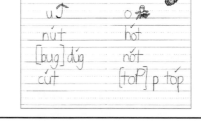

LEVEL 54	Print Book	Stepping Up	Reader	Skills Book
Red Word: *was*	94-95	46-49	9-12	5-9
Capital W				

Mom was not mad at Rags.
The ham was in the pot.
Tom was not at his job.
Was it hot in the sun?
Was Dot on the bus?
Was it fun to jog?

LEVEL 55	Stepping Up	Reader	Skills Book
e (elephant)	50-52	13-16	10-13

The use of the pocket chart can be discontinued after this level.

get	men	jet	fed
red	wet	pet	let
bed	pen	leg	web
yes	ten	met	yet

Ten men got on the jet.
Mom met us at ten.
Was Jim in bed?
Can a bug have six legs?
Did Ben's pets get fed yet?
Did you get the red pens?

After working with the new vowel for two or three lessons, do a divided dictation in which children have to distinguish between the vowels $\breve{i}$ and $\breve{e}$, which are the ones most often confused. Have the children fold their papers in half and write one vowel at the top of each column. Tell children to listen for the vowel sound and decide in which column to write each word. Dictate the following words: pet, pin, ten, pit, tin, pen.

i	e

LEVEL 56	Stepping Up	Reader	Skills Book
Suffix: -ing	53	17-20	14-16
(*doing* suffix)			

Introduce the terms *root word* and *suffix*. At this level the simplest explanation is that a suffix is one or more letters added to the end of a word to change the word's meaning. A root word is a word that has no suffix. You will do the review by asking the children, *What is the doing suffix*?

For spelling:
There are only four *-ing* words children are expected to spell at this level, because any other root words the children can spell would require doubling the final consonant, e.g., running, sitting.

Here's what you should do:
• Dictate the target word. *Fixing: He is fixing the broken bicycle.*

• Ask, W*hat is the root word in* fixing*?* Have the children write the root word (fix) on their papers.

• *Ask, What would you add to make it say* fixing*?* Have them add the suffix (-ing) to the written root word.

• Repeat the procedure for each of the words.

| mixing | waxing | boxing | fixing |

They are waxing the red bus.
The men are boxing.
Mom is fixing Kim's bed.
Is Ben fixing the bed's leg?
Is Mom mixing nuts yet?
Is Gus waxing his bus?

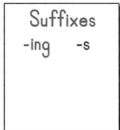

• When they are reading, have the children draw a line to separate the suffix.

     fix(ing

     wax(ing

• Read the root word and then the whole word as spoken (fix, fixing).

> Suffixes
> -ing   -s

• Eventually they can use their fingers to cover the suffix instead of drawing a pencil mark. This reading strategy is used to teach all suffixes in the sequence.

Begin your Suffix Chart, adding each suffix as it is taught. Divide the Suffix Chart into suffixes that begin with vowels (vowel suffixes) and those that begin with consonants (consonant suffixes) to help in the teaching of spelling rules later in the sequence.

LEVEL 57
Capital L

	Print Book	Stepping Up	Reader	Skills Book
	96-97	54	21-24	17-22

Let Ben have the red pen.
Lots of men are on the jet.
Logs can get wet.
Live it up.
Lots of dogs are big.
Let Ben run and get the bats.

LEVEL 58

Red Word: *from*

Capital O

	Print Book	Stepping Up	Reader	Skills Book
	98-99	55-56	25-28	23-26

I am hot from the sun.
Jim got the box from his mom.
Did you get the maps from the van?
Ben ran from his van to the bus.
Can a bug hop from log to log?
Did you get the gum from Tom?

Are you OK?
Mom said it was not OK to have nuts.
Is it OK to get on thc bus yet?
Was it OK to get wet?
It is not OK to pet a fox.
I said I am OK.

LEVEL 59

Capital E

-ll (for reading only)

	Print Book	Stepping Up	Reader	Skills Book
	100-101	57-58	29-32	28-30 (omit 27)

Tell children that when two of the same consonants appear together, they say the sound once, as in *hill*.

Ed's pen is red.
Ed was fixing the bus.
Ed was mixing the nuts.
Was Ed waxing the bus?
Have Ed and Tom met?
Did Ed get a job yet?

LEVEL 60

Capital U

-ff (for reading only)

	Print Book	Stepping Up	Reader	Skills Book
	102-103	59	33-36	31-34

Make sure the children know that USA stands for the United States of America.

Ed lives in the USA.
The USA is big.
Ed met Bob in the USA.
Ed has a map of the USA.
Are you from the USA?
They have a map of the USA.

LEVEL 61

	Stepping Up	Reader	Skills Book
	60-61	37-40	35-39

Red Word: *were*
-ss (for reading only)

> The men were fixing the bus.
> Ben's pets were in the mud.
> Ten men were on the bus.
> Were Ben and Ed boxing?
> Were the hens in the pen?
> Were his pens red?

LEVEL 62

	Print Book	Stepping Up	Reader	Skills Book
	104-105	62-63	41-44	40-43

Capital Z
Use of Exclamation Marks
-ck (for reading only)

Tell children that since *c* and *k* make the same sound, they need only say the sound once, as in *back*.

> Zap the hot dogs!
> Zip up the bag!
> Zigzags are fun to run.

LEVEL 63

	Print Book	Stepping Up	Reader	Skills Book
	106-107	64	45-48	44-47

Capital Qu
Final Double Consonants
(for reading only)

> Quit it!
> Quit your bad job.
> Quit waxing the van.

LEVEL 64

	Print Book	Stepping Up	Reader	Skills Book
	108-109	65-66	49-52	48-51

Capital V

> The pens were on the TV.
> The men were boxing on TV.
> Vans are big.
> Is it OK to put the box on top of the TV?
> Tom is fixing his TV.
> Ed has a big TV set.

LEVEL 65

	Print Book	Stepping Up	Reader	Skills Book
	110-111	67-68	53-56	52-57

Red Word: *very*
Suffix: -ed = /t/ (past time suffix)
(for reading only)

The suffix -ed makes three sounds: /id/, /d/, and /t/. The only reason that the suffix is presented at this level is because it appears in the reader. The suffix is not added to the review pack until the children start spelling words with this suffix at Level 92.

Kim was very mad at Tim!
Rags is a very big dog!
Ben got very wet in the mud.
Is Nat a very bad pet?
Were the hens very fat?
Were the kids very sad?

LEVEL 66
Compound Words

	Stepping Up	Reader	Skills Book
	69-70	57-60	58-61

Tell children that a compound word is a word made up of two smaller words.

Here's what you should do:
• Divide the words on an auditory level for the children as you dictate each word: *Write into, in-to.*

into	cannot	upset	laptop

Put your laptop into the box.
Was Dan very upset at Rags?
Ed said you cannot have his laptop.
Ben cannot fix Ed's TV.

• Show the children how to use their pencils to divide the words into two smaller words for reading.

up/set
lap/top

• Read each small word in sequence. Resay the word as spoken (*up-set, upset*).

LEVEL 67
th (thin)

	Stepping Up	Reader	Skills Book
	71	61-64	62-65

Some children have difficulty articulating /th/ and will need to be shown the correct placement of the tip of the tongue between the teeth. Teach the children that when they stick their tongues between their teeth, they will write the letters *th*.

Begin to use and display the Keyword Picture Cards.

thin	bath	them	then
with	this	that	bathtub
math			

Can Kim get on the bus with them?
Jim has to have a bath.
Is this laptop yours?
Dan cannot get Rags into the bathtub.
That bathtub is very big.
Ben's TV is very thin.

Take down the Alphabet Picture Cards and replace them with the Keyword Picture Cards as they are introduced. You may want to display a chart with the five vowels.

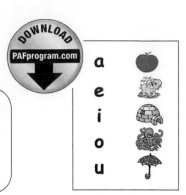

Vowel Chart

LEVEL 68
Red Word: *do*

	Stepping Up	Reader	Skills Book
	72	65-68	66-69

Mom can do this math with us.
Did you do math with your dad?
Do not run on the bus!
Do you live with them?
Do you have a laptop?
Do you give up?

LEVEL 69
Two-Letter Words (Long Vowel)
Red Word: *goes*

	Stepping Up	Reader	Skills Book
	73-75	69-72	71-74
			(omit 70)

Teach the children that the vowels *e* and *o* say their names at the end of these common two-letter words. That is why *to* and *do* are red words.

no	go	me	so
he	we	be	

We are going to jog with them.
He cannot go with us.
That is so sad!
Do not be so sad.
That bathtub has no suds in it.
He got so upset that he quit his job.

Red Word: *goes*

That jet goes to the USA.
He goes to bed at ten.
This rag goes in the bathtub.
He goes to math with me.
He goes to his job in a cab.
That big TV goes in the box.

LEVEL 70

		Stepping Up	Reader	Skills Book
ch (check)		76	73-76	75-78

-nch as in *lunch*

much	such	rich	chin
chop	chip		

He is a very rich man.
Chop that log with your ax.
That is such a thin pen.
We have so much math to do.
He got a bad cut on his chin.
We do not have that much to give you.

In order to read and spell several common words at this level, the children need extra practice with the final *-nch*.

lunch	punch	bunch	lunchbox
ranch	bench	pinch	

We sat on the bench and had lunch.
Dan's mom put chips in his lunchbox.
He had red punch with his lunch.
Do not punch me!
They live on a ranch.
He was mixing the punch himself.

LEVEL 71

	Stepping Up	Reader	Skills Book
Title: Mr.	77	77-80	79-82

An abbreviation is a shortened form of a word and is often followed by a period.

Mr. Rich had lunch with me.
Mr. Chin lives on a big ranch.
Mr. Chin cannot chop the logs.
Did Mr. Rich have chips with his lunch?
Is Mr. Chin a very rich man?
Did Mr. Rich have the punch?

LEVEL 72

	Stepping Up	Reader	Skills Book
-tch as in *catch* (for reading only)	78-79	81-84	83-85 (omit 86)

The *t* is silent.

LEVEL 73
-y (fly)

	Stepping Up	Reader	Skills Book
	80	85-88	87-90

The letter *y* is a consonant at the beginning of a word or syllable. At all other times, *y* is a vowel.

Teach the children that the sound /ī/ is spelled with the letter *y* at the end of a little word. The *y* is doing the job of a vowel.

        my   by

My mom sat on the red bench.
Put this bun in my lunchbox.
Rags had a nap by my bed.
Can Mr. Rich do my math with me?
Can you be at the bus by ten?
That is not my laptop.

You will find a sample lesson for this level on pages 202 to 204.

LEVEL 74
Title: Dr.

	Stepping Up	Reader	Skills Book
	81-82	89-91	91-95

Dr. Fox is a vet on TV.
Dr. Fox had lunch with Mr. Rich.
Dr. Fox is Nat's vet.
Can you get to Dr. Fox's ranch on the bus?
Is that Dr. Fox's lunchbox?
Dr. Fox has so much to do.

Time to stop teaching and give Proficiency Test #3.

> **Levels 75-96**
>
> Stepping Up In Reading 1
> Merrill Reader – Book D
> Merrill Skills Book D
> Keyword Picture Cards
> Review Pack I

Merrill Book D - *Get Set*

LEVEL 75

	Stepping Up	Reader	Skills Book
sh (ship)	83-84	5-7*	3-4*

she	ship	shop	shot
wish	shut	cash	shy
fish	dish	rush	

Dr. Fox gives Rags a shot.
Are you shy?
She goes fishing with them.
Did my mom give you a lot of cash?
The men on that ship are going fishing.
Put a lot of fish in my dish.

Follow up with a divided dictation in which the children choose between /ch/ and /sh/ using the following set of words: chip, wish, shut, ship, chop, dish, rich, shop, such.

I wish I were very rich.
Shut the lunchbox!
Put the chips in a dish.

LEVEL 76

	Stepping Up	Reader	Skills Book
Contractions	85-86	8-12	1, 2, 5

All the contractions in this lesson are formed using the word *not*.

isn't	didn't	haven't	aren't
wasn't	hasn't	weren't	

You want the children to know that in order to form contractions with the word *not*, they must replace the *o* in *not* with an apostrophe.

Here's what you should do:
• Write these words on the board:

> have not
> is not
> did not

*If you are using the 2016 version of the Merrill Reasers and Skills Books, the page numbers may be off by one page.

• Demonstrate how to cross out the *o* and substitute an apostrophe to write the contraction.

have nø̓t = haven't
is nø̓t = isn't
did nø̓t = didn't

Instead of doing a spelling dictation, give the children a work sheet with all seven contractions to practice the rule. The same sheet can be used for homework.

Two Words	Cross Out Letter(s)	Contraction
is not	is nø̓t	isn't
did not	did nø̓t	didn't
have not		
are not		

In a following lesson, give a spelling dictation with the contractions. Include the word *can't* which is an exception in that the apostrophe replaces both the letters *n* and *o*. Additional contractions will appear in the Readers and Skills Books and should be taught only for reading as they appear.

Jim can't go fishing with us.
She isn't so shy.
Aren't you going to shop?
That wasn't my laptop on the bench.
Mr. Rich hasn't had much lunch.
Dr. Fox didn't give Rags a shot.

LEVEL 77
Red Words: *don't, won't*

	Stepping Up	Reader	Skills Book
	87-88	13-18	6-10

Don't run with that dish!
Don't do that!
I don't have my lunchbox.
Don't be in such a rush!
Don't shut the van yet!
They don't have laptops in this shop.

I won't go fishing with you.
Mr. Rich won't go to the shop with me.
Won't you get hot in the sun?
Dr. Fox won't give Nat a shot.
The fish and chips won't fit in that dish.
She won't have lunch with us.

LEVEL 78		Stepping Up	Reader	Skills Book
-ang (gang)		89-90	19-24	11-16

-ong (song)
Red Word: *who*

The letters -*ng* make one sound, as in the word *hang*. The sound is difficult to hear without a vowel, and children often leave out the *n* when spelling these words. To make the spelling easier, you will teach these words as families, beginning with -*ang* and -*ong*.

bang	hang	sang	rang
long	song		

Don't bang the pans!
She wasn't hanging up the wet rags.
Won't you hang up your hat?
Mr. Rich sang a lot of songs with us.
That song wasn't very long.
An inch isn't very long.

Red Word: *who*

Who is banging the pans?
Who sang the song?
Who can go fishing with me?
Who are your pals?
Who is it?
Who is going to hang this up?

LEVEL 79		Stepping Up	Reader	Skills Book
-ing (ring)		91	25-30	17-21

Title: Ms.

king	wing	sing	thing
ring			

Do fish have wings?
Things aren't so bad.
Jets have long wings.
Ms. Long has six big rings!
Who was singing in the bathtub?
Ms. Long's things won't fit in that box.

LEVEL 80		Stepping Up	Reader	Skills Book
-ung (rungs)		92-93	31-36	22-26

Red Word: *school*

hung   rung

Ms. King hung up Dan's cap.
Go to the top rung to get that box.
I haven't hung up my hat yet.
Ms. King hung up on me.
It hasn't rung yet.
Have you hung up your things?

Red Word: *school*

Ms. King was rushing to the school bus.
We sang a lot of songs in school.
Jan goes to school with Tim.
Who said that Ms. King wasn't at school?
Don't you have fun at school?
That is a big school of fish by the ship.

LEVEL 81
Syllable Division: VCCV

	Stepping Up	Reader	Skills Book
	94-96	37-42	27-32

You will now begin teaching your students how to divide unfamiliar multisyllable words in order to read them. As the first lesson in syllabication, show your students how to divide two-syllable root words that contain the following sequence of letters: a vowel, followed by two consonants, followed by another vowel (VCCV). For example: **rabbi**t, **pic**nic, **unti**l. Later in the sequence, the children will learn VCV (m**u**sic) at Level 113 and VCCCV (comp**le**te) at Level 166. A summary of the three rules for dividing words can be found in the Appendix.

Here's what you should do:
• Write the following words on the board.

        picnic   magnet
        rabbit   lesson

• Tell the children that you are going to teach them a trick for reading big words. First, they will go on a vowel hunt and underline every vowel they can find.

        p<u>i</u>cn<u>i</u>c   m<u>a</u>gn<u>e</u>t
        r<u>a</u>bb<u>i</u>t   l<u>e</u>ss<u>o</u>n

• Next, search for pairs of consonants between two vowels and draw a line between them.

        p<u>i</u>c/n<u>i</u>c   mag/n<u>e</u>t
        r<u>a</u>b/b<u>i</u>t   l<u>e</u>s/s<u>o</u>n

• Last, they will read each syllable aloud, then say the whole word as it is spoken (*pic – nic, picnic*).

Have the students follow the same sequence (underline the vowels, divide between the two consonants, and read the word aloud) for the remaining three words. You will find lists of two-syllable words to use for practice in Stepping Up.

LEVEL 82

Suffix: -es

	Stepping Up	Reader	Skills Book
	97-98	43-48	33-37

The suffix -es has two meanings: it forms plurals, and it is a verb form. Tell the children that when they hear /ĭz/ at the end of a root word, it is spelled *-es*. For simplicity, the suffix is reviewed by asking children to write the suffix that says /ĭz/, as in *wishes*. Add -es to the Suffix Chart.

boxes	fixes	dishes	lunches
mixes	inches	rushes	waxes

Ms. King didn't have the lunches.
That fish isn't ten inches long.
Put the dishes in the boxes.
Ms. King rushes to the school bus.
Who waxes Ben's van?
Ms. King fixes the TV.

LEVEL 83

-lf (elf)
-nd (hand)

	Stepping Up	Reader	Skills Book
	99	49-52	38-45

A blend is two or three consonants blended together, as in the words *fast* and *stop*. Each consonant sound can be heard. Book D contains many final blends, and Book E contains initial blends.

shelf	myself	himself	yourself

Ms. Chin put the boxes on the shelf.
Ms. Long said to do your math by yourself.
Gus hung the shelf by himself.
Mr. Rich waxes his van by himself.
I am going to hang up the shelf by myself.
Can you fix the benches by yourself?

and	send	hand	band
end	bend	sand	lend
land	pond	wind	sandbox

Didn't the jet land yet?
Who is in the school band?
Is that the end of that long song?
Can Mr. Sands lend you a laptop?
Mr. Sands fishes in the pond.
Can you give me a hand with this shelf?

Add each final blend to the review pack. Keep and review the blends separately from the other phonograms. You will do the review of blends slightly differently, because blends can be difficult to hear in isolation. Ask the children to write the blend at the end of the keyword. For example, *Write the blend you hear at the end of the word* elf. Children respond by saying and skywriting the blend.

LEVEL 84
Title: Mrs.

Stepping Up	Reader	Skills Book
100-101	53-60	46-48

Who has Mrs. Chin's lunch?
Hand in your math to Mrs. Sands.
Mrs. Sands can send the boxes to school.
Mrs. Sands will fix the benches by the pond.
Are Mr. and Mrs. Chin in the band?
Mrs. Chin said to fix the sandbox yourself.

LEVEL 85
-nt (tent)

Stepping Up	Reader	Skills Book
102-103	61-63	49, 51-53
		(omit 50)

ant	hunt	sent	lent
went	tent	rent	pants

Gus Sands lent us his tent.
I didn't hang up my pants yet.
Mrs. Sands is renting a van.
We have a lot of ants in the sandbox.
Who went hunting with Mr. Sands?
My mom sent me to shop by myself.

Time to stop teaching and give Proficiency Test #4.

LEVEL 86
Suffix: -er
(*doer* suffix)

Stepping Up	Reader	Skills Book
104-105	64-66	54-55

The suffix -er has two meanings: it means a person or thing that does something (*singer*) or it can mean more (*faster*). In this lesson you will teach the children the first meaning. Review the suffix by asking, *What is* the doer *suffix?* Add -er to your Suffix Chart.

boxer	hunter	punter	rancher
mixer	singer	golfer	sander

The boxers went into the ring.
Who is that singer?
Dot says she can't fix the mixer.
The hunters set up a tent by the pond.
Isn't Mrs. Sands a golfer?
Ben has to rent a sander to fix the shelf.

LEVEL 87

-ank (bank)
-ink (pink)
-unk (trunk)

		Stepping Up	Reader	Skills Book
		106-107	67-72	56-63

bank	sank	tank	yank
thank			

Thank you very much!
Mrs. Banks went to the bank to get cash.
Mr. Banks is a rich banker.
The ship sank in the pond.
Give the top of the box a yank.
We have a tank of fish at school.

ink	wink	sink	pink
think			

Put the dishes in the sink.
The box was sinking in the pond.
I think I can do it myself.
This pen has pink ink.
Don't wink at me!
Mrs. Sands thinks she can go to the bank.

junk	chunk	bunk	dunk
sunk			

Jim and Kim have bunk beds.
That junk has got to go!
Mrs. Banks got rid of a lot of junk.
Can I have a chunk of that?
My fishing rod sunk in the pond.
Don't dunk the chips in your mug!

LEVEL 88

-st (west)

		Stepping Up	Reader	Skills Book
		108-109	73-78	64-68

fast	must	nest	test
just	list	last	dust
best	west	rest	chest

The sun is sinking in the west.
Did you dust the chest yet?
I must get to school fast.
Mrs. Banks has a long list of things to do.
Who do you think is the best singer?
We just had a math test.

LEVEL 89
Suffix: -er
(comparative *more*)

	Stepping Up	Reader	Skills Book
	110-111	79-84	70-72
			(omit 69)

This is the second meaning of the suffix -er. Review the suffix by alternating the meanings: one day ask for the *doer* suffix, and the next day ask for the suffix that means *more.* Children often confuse *then* and *than.* Be sure to pronounce *than* clearly in the sentences.

faster   longer   richer   pinker

Dan can't run faster than his dad.
Is Ben richer than Gus Sands?
The fish is ten inches longer than yours.
The wind won't last much longer.
My pants are pinker than my tank top.
He wishes he was richer than a king.

LEVEL 90
-sk (mask)
-ft (gift)

	Stepping Up	Reader	Skills Book
	112-113	85-87	73-76

ask   desk   mask

Did you fix the desk yourself?
Ask your mom if you can go with us.
Pam's mask is red and pink.
Sit at your desk and do the test.
Ask Dan if he can run faster than Jim.
Put the masks on my desk.

left   gift   lift   raft
soft

Jim put the pen in his left hand.
Kim left the gift in Ben's van.
I think sand can be very soft.
Ask your mom if we can go rafting.
Lift up your left hand.
My hands are softer than his.

LEVEL 91
-er as in *after*
(for reading only)

	Stepping Up	Reader	Skills Book
	114-115	88-90	77-79

Children will now learn to read two-syllable root words containing /er/ as an ending sound, rather than as a suffix, for example, *after, thunder, number.*

Write these words on the board and use them to review how to divide VCCV words.

af/ter   num/ber
thun/der   sil/ver

You will find lists of two-syllable words for practice in Stepping Up.

LEVEL 92

	Stepping Up	Reader	Skills Book
	116	91-93	80-81

Suffix: -ed = /ĭd/
(past time suffix)

You will review -ed by asking the children, *What is the past time suffix?* Because this suffix makes more than one sound, the children reply by naming the letters, *e, d.*

lifted	landed	handed	dented
rested	ended	rented	listed

Jim rested on Kim's bunk bed.
Mr. and Mrs. Banks rented a van.
The jet hasn't landed yet.
Ms. Sands handed me a gift.
Dad lifted the kids onto the raft.
We left just as the song ended.

LEVEL 93

	Stepping Up	Reader	Skills Book
	117-118	94-96	82-84

Red Word: *want*

I don't want to go hunting.
Ms. King didn't want us to do math yet.
Ask Gus if he wants to go by himself.
Who wants to go rafting?
Ben wanted to get his mom a gift.
My dad wanted to be a singer.

Want, went and *won't* are often confused in spelling. Remind children that they can hear the /ĕ/ in *went* and the /ō/ in *won't*. Try some of these sentences in subsequent dictations.

I won't want to go to the pond with them.
Mom went to get the gift that Pam wants.
I want fish so my mom went to get it.
The kids went fishing so they want to rest.
I won't ask Kim if she wants to go.
The hunter won't want to set up his tent in the wind.

LEVEL 94

	Stepping Up	Reader	Skills Book
	119-120	97-99	88-89
			(omit 85)

-lt (belt)
-lk (milk)

belt	melt	quilt	felt

She can't fit your belt on the pants.
Mrs. Sands felt rested.
Mom is mending the quilt.
It hasn't melted yet.
The quilt wasn't as big as the bed.
Pam felt the soft quilt and wanted it.

silk	hulk	milk	elk

Ms. King wants milk with lunch.
Can an elk run very fast?
A hulk is a very big thing.
Put the silk quilt on the bed.
Don't dunk the chips in your milk!
The boxer was a hulk of a man.

LEVEL 95

	Stepping Up	Reader	Skills Book
-mp (stamp)	121-122	100-102	86-87

jump	camp	bump	dump
lamp			

Include these common words with final blends:

help	next

Can you help me lift this lamp?
Ben isn't going to camp.
Don't jump on the bunk bed!
Put the mugs next to the dishes.
Don't dump that junk on my quilt!
The jet landed with a bump.

LEVEL 96

	Stepping Up	Reader	Skills Book
Suffix: -ed = /t/	123-124	103-107	90-95
(past time suffix)			

Tell the children that they are going to spell some words with the past time suffix -ed, but the suffix is going to make the sound /t/.

mixed	wished	thanked	fixed
helped	asked	jumped	rushed

Jim helped me so I thanked him.
We wished we didn't have so much math to do.
Mr. Rich jumped up and helped me lift the TV.
Mr. Sands fixed his bus by himself.
Mrs. Banks mixed up the boxes.
Ms. King asked if we were going camping.

Time to stop teaching and give Proficiency Test #5.

> **Levels 97-129**
>
> Stepping Up In Reading 2
> Merrill Reader – Book E
> Merrill Skills Book E
> Keyword Picture Cards
> Review Pack I

Merrill Book E - *Step Up*

LEVEL 97	Stepping Up	Reader	Skills Book
Open and Closed Syllables	1-2	—	—

You will now begin teaching your students the six different syllable types: open, closed, r-controlled, silent e, vowel team, and special syllable endings. A description of all six syllable types can be found in the Appendix. For the first lesson you will teach open and closed syllables.

An open syllable is one that ends with a vowel, and the vowel sound is long (this means the vowel says its name as in prē, cō, bī). When an open syllable ends with the letter *u*, the *u* says /ū/ as in *music,* or /o͞o/ as in *tulip*). A closed syllable ends with a consonant, and the vowel sound is short (cŏn, ŭn, mĕnt). The critical concept for your students to learn at this level is that the way to determine whether the vowel sound is long or short is to look at the last letter of the syllable. If the last letter of the syllable is a vowel, the vowel is long; if the last letter is a consonant, the vowel is short. This simple strategy will allow your students to divide and decode unfamiliar words as they begin to read independently.

Day 1
Here is what you should do:
• Put a list of open syllables on the board, with the final letter in color.

> ta
> re
> si
> bo
> mu

• Have the children look at the syllables to see what they have in common. (In this case, all the syllables end with vowels.)

• Read the syllables aloud to the children and use each syllable in a word (tā as in *table*, rē as in *remember*). Ask the children what the vowels are saying in these syllables: *Are the vowels saying their names, or are they making their regular sounds?* Here the vowels are saying their names: *We call a vowel that says its name a **long** vowel.*

• Help the children formulate the rule that when they see a vowel at the end of a syllable, the vowel will say its name.

- Repeat this procedure with closed syllables. Now, the syllables will all end with consonants, and the vowels will make their regular, or **short**, sound.

>   ha**p**
>   e**x**
>   ri**v**
>   co**n**
>   u**n**

For this introductory lesson on syllable types, you do not need to give a spelling dictation. Instead, have the children go directly to page 1 in Stepping Up, where they can practice reading open and closed syllables. The words on page 1 have been divided into syllables, so the children just need to look at the last letter of each syllable to decide the vowel sound. Have a child read a word by reading each of its syllables, and then repeating the word as it is normally spoken (*hu-man, human*). Only by pronouncing the word as it is commonly spoken can a child understand its meaning. It is not necessary for the students to label the syllables as open or closed as long as they can read the word correctly.

Day 2

For the second lesson on open and closed syllables, you will give a spelling dictation that includes detached syllables and two-syllable words. Download and use this form for the dictation.

Here is what to do:

- Dictate three or four open syllables, using each syllable in a word. For example, say: *Write /rē/, as in* **re**member.

mu	u	ze	o
mo	e	si	hu
ro	tu	co	ba

- Dictate three or four closed syllables, again using each syllable in a word. For example, say: *Write /ŭn/, as in* **un**derstand. (FYI: The sound /k/ is always spelled with a *c* at the end of a syllable, as in *picnic*.)

ven	ish	sic	sev
ment	gan	vis	bot
en	ond	ex	ic

Name Sam

Dictate detached syllables.

ro si ze mu
gan ven bot sic

First Syllable	Second Syllable	Word
ro	bot	robot ✓
fin	ish	finish ✓
si	lent	silent ✓
ze	ro	zero ✓
vis	it	visit ✓

- Before you dictate two-syllable words, make sure the children understand what they will need to do on their papers. First, they will write the first syllable of each word in the first column, then the second syllable in the second column, and finally the whole word in the last column.

- Dictate a word and use it in a sentence. For example, say: *Write* robot. *The boy played with his toy robot.*

- Model breaking the word *robot* into syllables for the children: *robot, ro-bot.*

• Dictate four more words modeling how to break the word into syllables.

• Tell the children that you will now say a word and they will have to break it into syllables themselves. Dictate five more words.

begin	picnic	zero	finish
music	began	visit	moment
hero	second	robot	open
until	robin	menu	seven
human	belong	silent	even

Although the words *open, seven,* and *even* are not taught until Level 159 (-en), they are included for spelling at this earlier level because they are so common. When dictating each of these words, be sure to emphasize the short e sound in the second syllable, *o-pĕn.* Otherwise, children are likely to spell the word with an *i.*

LEVEL 98	Stepping Up	Reader	Skills Book
pl- (plant)	3-4	5-8*	2-3*
Red Word: *what*			(omit 1)

This is the first initial blend. As you teach each initial blend, add it to the review pack.

plan	plus	plant	plastic

Six plus zero is six.
We can't plant until we get the plastic pots.
The kids finished planting.
We have to plan the lunch menu.
Put the milk in the plastic cups.
Do you plan to help me finish planting?

Red Word: *what*

What are your plans?
What do you want to do next?
What is seven plus zero?
What do you want to do until lunch?
What did you want to ask me?
What is on the menu?

LEVEL 99	Stepping Up	Reader	Skills Book
gl- (glass)	5-6	9-10	4-5

glad	glum	glob

We were glad to help you.
We asked Max if he felt glum.

---

*If you are using the 2016 version of the Merrill Reasers and Skills Books, the page numbers may be off by one page.

I am glad we finished planting.
Even a hero can be glum.
Mr. Sands has globs of mud on his pants.
We were glad Ms. King visited.

LEVEL 100
bl- (black)

		Stepping Up	Reader	Skills Book
		7	11-13	6-8

blink   blank   blond   blast

A blast is a big gust of wind.
What goes in the blank?
The school picnic was a blast!
Who is that blond kid?
Do you blink a lot in the sun?
We blinked in the gust of wind.

LEVEL 101
Red Words: *one, done, none*

	Stepping Up	Reader	Skills Book
	8-10	14-16	9-10

Can one of you help me fix the desk?
The kids got on the bus one by one.
Six plus one is seven.
We can begin in one moment.

Are they done blasting yet?
What have you done with the boxes?
We thanked Ms. King after she was done helping us.
We can go if you are done with your math.

None of us wanted to do the dishes.
None of this junk belongs to me.
I think none of the plants are up yet.
None of the kids were finished.

LEVEL 102
cl- (clock)
Red Word: *there*

	Stepping Up	Reader	Skills Book
	11-12	17-19	11-13

club   clip   clap   clam

Clams live in sand and mud.
Do you belong to the math club?
Put the clips on Ms. King's desk.
Do you want six clams?
That golf club belongs to me.
The kids began to clap after the singers were done.

Red Word: *there*

The word *there* introduces a sentence that tells a fact and is often followed by the words *is, are, was,* or *were*. Put up the following chart, whose purpose is to familiarize the children with the correct spelling of *there* in these phrases.

There is a music club at his school.
There is a box of clips on the desk.
There are ten kids in the math club.
There was a bug in my milk!
There are six golf clubs in my bag.
There were seven robins in the nest.

> There is...
> There are...
> There was...
> There were...

LEVEL 103
ar (star)

	Stepping Up	Reader	Skills Book
	13-15	20-22	14-16

When the letter *r* follows a vowel, the vowel is usually forced to change its sound (Bossy R). The vowel and the letter *r* make a new vowel sound, called an r-controlled vowel (ar, or, er, ir, ur).

car	farm	yard	March
arm	hard	dark	sharp
jar	barn	harm	carve
card	park	march	shark

We won't visit the farm until next March.
The barn was dark and silent.
The farmer parked his car next to the barn.
The band marches in the school yard.
None of us wanted to go to the park.
There is one open jar of jam on the shelf.

LEVEL 104
sl- (sleep)
Red Words: *some, come*

	Stepping Up	Reader	Skills Book
	16-18	23-25	18-20
			(omit 17)

sled	slip	slid	sly
sling	slim	slush	slant

Mark's arm is in a sling until it mends.
The sly fox ran into the barnyard.
Did you slip in the slush?
Mark's sled slid into a parked car.
That man is very slim.
Do you want to get your sled and go to the park?

Red Words: *some, come*

Some sharks are as big as a bus.
There are some cars parked next to the barn.
Some of the kids visited a farm.
Mark left some open jars on the top shelf.
There is someone marching in the yard.
Mark wants something sharp to carve the ham.

Can you come to the park with me after school?
Did someone come with you in Mark's car?
Come help me carve the ham.
Ask your mom if you can come to the picnic.
Come and help us put up the charts.
I am so glad you can come to the farm with me.

LEVEL 105

	Stepping Up	Reader	Skills Book
	19-20	26-28	21-23

Suffix: -est
(comparative *most*)

Review this suffix by asking, *What is the suffix that means* the most? Add -est to your Suffix Chart.

fastest	hardest	longest	darkest
sharpest	softest		

That was the hardest math test ever!
Mark's car is the fastest one.
That is the softest silk I have ever felt.
Give me the sharpest one you have.
I want the pen with the darkest red ink.
Is that shark the longest one in the tank?

LEVEL 106

	Stepping Up	Reader	Skills Book
	21-22	29-31	24-27

fl- (flag)

flag	flap	flu	flash
flat	fly	flip	flex

The flag flaps in the wind.
There were seven bats flying in the barn.
The boxer flexed his arms.
The car's blinkers were flashing.
The robin flaps its wings.
Mark's car hit something sharp and got a flat.

LEVEL 107
sm- (smile)
sn- (snail)

	Stepping Up	Reader	Skills Book
	23-24	32-36	28-31

smart   smash   smog

Is it hard to fly jets in smog?
I think I have the smartest dog.
Don't smash the dishes!
Smog can harm your lungs.
It isn't smart to go to the park in the dark.
Mark smashed his car and dented it.

snap   snug   snip   snob

Snap your fingers to the music.
Snip your bangs so they aren't so long.
Don't be such a snob!
I felt as snug as a bug in a rug.
The snap on your pants is open!
My pants felt very snug.

LEVEL 108
sp- (spot)
spl- (for reading only)

	Stepping Up	Reader	Skills Book
	25-26	37-40	32, 34

spot   spin   spend   spent
spy   spark

I spent a lot of cash on Mark's gift.
A spy must be smart.
Give the top a spin.
Did the sparks fly onto the rug?
It is not smart to spend all your cash.
There was one parking spot next to the school.

LEVEL 109
or (corn)

	Stepping Up	Reader	Skills Book
	27-29	41-42	33, 35-36

or   born   short   forget
for   fork   north   forgive
corn   porch   sport   popcorn

What sports are you fond of?
North is at the top of maps.
There is a red sports car parked next to the van.
Forgive me for bumping into you.
Was Mark's visit long or short?
Some chipmunks live under the porch.

LEVEL 110

	Stepping Up	Reader	Skills Book
R-controlled Syllables	30-31	43-45	37-39

You will now teach your students the third syllable type, r-controlled syllables. An r-controlled syllable ends with the letter *r*, and the vowel will make its Bossy R sound (gar, morn, ber). At this level your students will be learning r-controlled syllables that contain ar, or, and er. (They will learn ur at Level 179 and ir at Level 181.) After teaching these r-controlled syllables, you will have your students practice reading them in two-syllable words (morning, barber).

The critical concept for your students to learn at this level is that if the last letter of a syllable is an *r*, the vowel will make its Bossy R sound and will not be long or short. As with open and closed syllables, the children should look at the last letter of the syllable to determine the vowel sound.

Day 1
Here is what you should do:
• Put a list of r-controlled syllables on the board with the final letter in color.

> mar
> per
> tor
> der
> cor

• Have the children look at the syllables to see what they have in common. (All the syllables end with *r*.)

• Read the syllables to the children and use each syllable in a word (*mar* as in *marble*). Ask the children what the vowels are saying in these syllables. (The vowels are saying their Bossy R sounds.)

• Help them formulate the rule that when they see *r* at the end of a syllable, the vowel will make its Bossy R sound.

• For this introductory lesson on r-controlled syllables, use the same form you downloaded at Level 97 for the spelling dictation. Dictate five or six r-controlled syllables, for example: *Write* gar*, as in* garden.

cor	gar	der	ar
ter	morn	har	ver

• Dictate a word and use it in a sentence, for example: *Write* number. *Six is an even number.* Do not divide the words into syllables for the children. By this point, they should be breaking words into syllables by themselves in order to spell them.

• Dictate nine more words from the list on the following page.

Day 2

The next spelling dictation will consist of words and sentences and is done on the children's usual writing paper rather than the downloaded form.

number	under	winter	barber
after	sister	morning	river
corner	tiger	paper	ever
over	super	never	spider

The barbershop on the corner is super.
Is winter over yet?
There are big spiders under the porch.
Who asked for the morning paper?
Six is an even number.
Some sharks live in rivers.

Even though the children are not spelling three-syllable root words yet, you may want to have them spell the months September, October, and November, which are composed of open, closed, and r-controlled syllables.

LEVEL 111

	Stepping Up	Reader	Skills Book
all (ball)	32-34	46-48	40-41

all	ball	hall	mall
call	tall	fall	small
wall			

Is your sister taller or shorter than you are?
Do you want to go to the mall this morning?
Who just hit that ball over the wall?
Winter comes after fall.
Never run in the halls.
What do you call a small pig?

LEVEL 112

	Stepping Up	Reader	Skills Book
st- (stop)	35-36	49-51	43-44
Red Word: *off*			(omit 42)

stop	start	step	star
storm	stamp	stand	

A star is a big ball of gas.
I can't stand going to malls.
That was some storm this morning!
Stop messing up my paper!
Don't forget to get stamps to send the cards.
The school clubs won't start until the fall.

Red Word: *off*

Don't fall off the wall!
Do you want the TV on or off?
We have to get off the bus at the next stop.
Did the spots come off your shorts?
Get this fly off me!
They put off going to the mall until one.

Time to stop teaching and give Proficiency Test #6.

LEVEL 113	Stepping Up	Reader	Skills Book
Syllable Division: VCV	37-38	52-54	45-47

You will now teach the children how to divide unfamiliar multisyllable words that contain the following sequence of letters: one vowel, followed by one consonant, followed by another vowel (VCV). For example: m**u**si**c**, sp**ider**, s**eve**n. Words that follow the VCV pattern are usually divided after the first vowel (be/gin) unless dividing it that way does not produce a word. In that case, the word is divided after the consonant (vis/it).

Here's what you should do:
• Write the following words on the board.

          moment   super
          tiger   music

• Tell the children to go on a vowel hunt and underline every vowel they can find.

          m<u>o</u>m<u>e</u>nt   s<u>u</u>p<u>e</u>r
          t<u>i</u>g<u>e</u>r   m<u>u</u>s<u>i</u>c

• Ask the children, *What will we do with only one consonant, not two, between the vowels?* Tell them they should always start by dividing after the first vowel, because most words fit this pattern.

          m<u>o</u>/m<u>e</u>nt   s<u>u</u>/p<u>e</u>r
          t<u>i</u>/g<u>e</u>r   m<u>u</u>/s<u>i</u>c

• Sometimes dividing after the first vowel does not produce a word (se/ven, fi/nish). In this case, tell the children to move over one letter and divide after the first consonant. Have them try to read the word again (sev/en, fin/ish). This division changes the vowel from long to short and produces a word.

Have the students follow the same sequence (underline the vowels, divide after the vowel and try reading the word aloud, changing the division if necessary) for the remaining words. You will find lists of two-syllable words to use for practice in Stepping Up.

LEVEL 114
-ll

	Stepping Up	Reader	Skills Book
	39-40	55-57	49-50

Many spelling patterns follow the principle that a short vowel sometimes needs an extra letter. For example, in these one-syllable words, the final *l* is doubled after the short vowels.

will	fell	pill	spill
tell	bell	doll	spell
well	dull	yell	smell
hill	sell	fill	still

Fill in all the blanks on the paper.
Someone will tell us if the bell rings.
I will start my spelling in one moment.
Bill sells dolls at his shop.
Mom never yells at us if we spill milk.
The pills are next to the sink.

LEVEL 115
Suffix: -ed=/d/
(past time suffix)

	Stepping Up	Reader	Skills Book
	41-42	58-60	48, 51-52

This is the third and last pronunciation of the suffix -ed.

yelled	filled	spilled	opened
smelled	called	harmed	

No one was harmed in the storm.
All the milk smelled bad.
The yard was filled with mud.
Don't forget to tell Bill that his sister called.
Jill ran and yelled for the ball.
Someone fell and spilled the popcorn.

LEVEL 116
sk- (skunk)

	Stepping Up	Reader	Skills Book
	43-44	61-64	54-55
			(omit 53)

sky	skip	skin	skunk

Skunks can smell very bad.
The sky was still and dark after the storm.
All the stars lit up the dark sky.
Is it faster to skip or run?
Don't skip lunch.
He will yell if he thinks he smells a skunk.

LEVEL 117

sw- (swing)
Red Words: *walk, talk*

	Stepping Up	Reader	Skills Book
	45-46	65-67	56-59

swim	swam	swing	swell

We put up a swing set in the yard.
Fish have fins that help them swim.
The kids swam in the river all morning.
Bill banged his leg and it swelled up.
Jill did a swell job on the spelling test.
Do you think it is smart to swim with sharks?

Red Words: *walk, talk*

We will all go for a long walk in the park.
Who will walk the dog?
Do you want to walk to school with us in the fall?
Don't ever go walking in a bad storm.
Bill was swinging his arms as he walked.
Jill walked to the river for a swim.

Jill wants to talk to Dr. Parker.
Bill's sister can't talk yet.
Don't talk after the bell rings.
Did Ms. Miller give Jill a doll that talks?
We all sat on the porch talking.
Jill talked Bill into going for a walk.

LEVEL 118

-ss
Title: Miss

	Stepping Up	Reader	Skills Book
	47	68-70	60-63

This is another spelling pattern in which a short vowel needs an extra letter. In these one-syllable words, the final *s* is doubled after the short vowels.

kiss	mess	less	boss
miss	pass	class	glass

Put all the dishes and glasses in the sink.
Someone messed up all my papers!
Is seven less than six?
My glasses are still missing.
Miss Smith is going to have a talk with her class.
My boss thinks I do a super job.

LEVEL 119

tw- (twelve)

Red Word: *where*

	Stepping Up	Reader	Skills Book
	48-49	71-73	64-65

twig	twin	twist	twelve

Is twelve an even number?
Six plus six is twelve.
Jill twisted the cap off the jar.
I passed my twin sister in the hall.
The long path twisted up the hill.
Are Miss Smith and Mrs. Parker twins?

Red Word: *where*

Where do the twins live?
Where did you go walking?
Where are we going?
Tell me where you put my pills.
I forgot where I put my glasses.
None of the papers are where they belong.

LEVEL 120

tr- (truck)

str- (for reading only)

	Stepping Up	Reader	Skills Book
	50-51	74-76	66-68

try	trot	trim	trust
trip	trap	trunk	trash

What were you trying to do?
I think he will try to do his best.
Don't slam the trunk of the car.
Spiders have webs to trap bugs.
We will rent a van for the trip.
Where do you want me to put the trash?

LEVEL 121

cr- (crab)

scr- (for reading only)

	Stepping Up	Reader	Skills Book
	52	77-79	69, 71-72
			(omit 70)

cry	crab	crash	cross
crib	crush	crust	crisp

Don't cry over spilled milk.
A crab has a hard shell.
The crust was very crisp.
A crib is a bed with bars.
Did Bill's car crash into the wall?
We crossed the parking lot to get to the car.

LEVEL 122

	Stepping Up	Reader	Skills Book
-ff	53	80-82	73

Once again the short vowel needs an extra letter. In these one-syllable words, the final *f* is doubled after the short vowels.

cuff	stiff	cliff	stuff
puff	sniff		

Something that is stiff is hard to bend.
Jeff puffed as he ran up the cliff.
The trunks were stuffed with junk.
The dog started sniffing at the cuff of Jeff's pants.
Do you want to put the stuffing in this dish?
Jeff got his dad silver cuff links.

LEVEL 123

	Stepping Up	Reader	Skills Book
fr- (frog)	54-55	83-88	74-75, 79
Red Word: *friend*			

frog	fry	fresh	frost

Frogs live in ponds.
The popcorn was hot and fresh.
Do you want to fry this fresh fish?
Put some fresh corn in the stuffing.
That frog has small spots.
There was frost on all the plants this morning.

Red Word: *friend*

A friend is someone you trust.
Can my friends come over after school?
Do you walk to school with your friends?
Jeff spent last March visiting friends.
Who is your best friend?
I am glad that you are my friend.

LEVEL 124

	Stepping Up	Reader	Skills Book
dr- (drum)	56	89-91	76-77

dry	drop	drag	drink
drum	drip	dress	drill

Stop banging on the drums!
I finished drinking my glass of milk.
Can you drag Jeff's sled up to the cliff?
One of the snaps on your dress is open.

Did you finish drying the frying pan?
Try not to drip the milk as you walk.

LEVEL 125	Stepping Up	Reader	Skills Book
gr- (green)	57	92-94	80-84

From this point on, you will need to tell the children when compound words appear in sentences. They are no longer included on the word lists.

grin	grass	grand	grandkids
grab	grill		

Jeff hit a grand slam over the ballpark wall.
Don't drop the trash on the grass!
Have you ever grilled fresh corn?
My friend had a big grin after she opened her gift.
Grandkids are so much fun!
Can you grab my bags for me?

LEVEL 126	Stepping Up	Reader	Skills Book
br- (brush)	58	95-97	86-87
			(omit 85)

brag	brush	brand	branch
bring			

Who is bringing the bats and balls to the ballpark?
Branches can snap in a storm.
Don't brag to your friends.
Can you bring some fresh corn to grill?
Rub the grill with a hard brush.
What brand of milk do you drink?

LEVEL 127	Stepping Up	Reader	Skills Book
pr- (pretzel)	59-60	98-100	88-89
spr- (for reading only)			

print	press	pretend	April

April comes after March.
Bill will print the spelling list for the class.
Can you bring your dad's pants to be pressed?
Some of the bulbs will come up in April.
My friend put some paper in his printer.
Do you want to dress up and pretend to be kings?

LEVEL 128
Red Word: *full*

	Stepping Up	Reader	Skills Book
	61-62	101-104	91-94

We all felt full after lunch.
This path is full of twists.
Aren't you full yet?
The sky is full of stars.
Is the car's trunk full of boxes?
The robin's nest is full of eggs.

LEVEL 129
Suffixes: -ful (full of)
         -less (without)

	Stepping Up	Reader	Skills Book
	63-66	105-107	90, 95

thankful   harmful   handful   helpful

I am thankful for your help.
Try to be helpful.
Bill pressed a handful of nuts into the mix.
Fixing the printer was very helpful.
Is it harmful for humans to live with smog?
What are some things you are thankful for?

endless   harmless   spotless

It was just a harmless spider.
Do you think tiger cubs are harmless?
The long car trip felt endless.
Rub the grill until it is spotless.
Don't mess up the spotless sink.
Last winter felt endless to me.

> Mark
>
> -ful -ful -ful
> thankful harmful
> handful helpful
> -less -less -less
> endless harmless spotless
> ✱ What are some things
> you are thankful for?
> ✱ The long car trip felt
> endless.

Time to stop teaching and give Proficiency Test #7.

Levels 130-158

Stepping Up In Reading 2
Merrill Reader – Book F
Merrill Skills Book F
Keyword Picture Cards
Review Pack II

Merrill Book F - *Lift Off*

Book F presents some new challenges for your students. Until now, the children have been learning letters and letter combinations for which there is just one sound, such as p=/p/ or sh=/sh/. Now they will learn that some sounds can be spelled in multiple ways. For example, all the common long vowels can be spelled with a magic *e* that is silent (*cake, hike*) or by using a vowel team (*rain, leaf*).

In order to spell words with long vowel sounds, your students will need to choose the correct spelling from a number of possibilities. There are common spelling patterns that you can teach your class that will help them make reasonable choices. Certain phonograms come only at the beginning or middle of a word, such as *oa* (*boat*), while others come at the end of a word, such as *ow* (*snow*). With these patterns in mind, the children can figure out which phonogram to use when they do not remember how a word is spelled. For example, with the word *throw,* they would sound out the initial consonants, then choose *ow* for the /ō/ sound, because it comes at the end of the word.

To help the children learn the various ways to spell long vowel sounds, you should display Spelling Choice Charts in your classroom. Using these charts, the children can make reasonable spelling choices when they do not know how to spell a word. After teaching each long vowel phonogram, add it to the chart. By the end of Book F, your charts will look like this:

Children with poor visual memories often have trouble memorizing words by sight. For instance, when asked to spell a word like *teach,* these students may struggle to remember whether to use *ee* or *ea,* and there is no rule for how to make this choice. On the other hand, children with good visual memories are likely to remember how the word looks in print and thus make the correct spelling choice, *ea.* Keep in mind that with your struggling spellers, what is most important is that their spelling choices be reasonable. It is reasonable to spell long *e* in the middle of a word with an *ee* or *ea*, not with an *e* or *y.* As long as your students can make reasonable spelling choices, their writing can be understood and corrected.

Remember, PAF is a reading program. Reading accuracy, fluency, and comprehension are the primary goals. At this point in the sequence, be careful not to slow down to work on spelling. Do not forget that reading, not spelling, should determine the pace of instruction. When your students have finished the Merrill Readers and start reading chapter books, you can revisit earlier lessons in the sequence to work on spelling.

LEVEL 130	Stepping Up	Reader	Skills Book
a-e (snake)	67-69	5-7*	1-4*

This is the first of five lessons on magic *e,* in which a silent *e* at the end of the word changes the vowel sound from short to long. The words end with a vowel followed by a consonant and an *e* (a-e, i-e, o-e, u-e, e-e; the hyphen stands for a consonant). There are a few words, such as *taste* and *bathe,* in which two consonants come between the vowel and the magic *e.* These words, however, are rare.

So far the children have learned one spelling of long *a, a* as in *paper* (an open syllable). Now you will teach them that *a-e* spells /ā/, as in *snake.*

Download the Spelling Choice Chart for long *a* with the first of two spellings visible.

Here is what you should do:
• Put the following list of words on the board with the vowels in color.

> mad
>
> can
>
> at
>
> cap
>
> plan

• Ask a child to read the first word, *mad.*

• Add an *e* to the word (in color). Tell the children: *This is a magic* e. *It is silent, but it does something tricky to the vowel. It makes the vowel say its name. Now the word says* made.

• Cover the *e* and have a child read the word. Uncover the *e* and read the new word.

• Repeat this procedure with the other four words.

• Help the children formulate the rule that adding a magic *e* to the end of a word changes the vowel sound from short to long.

*If you are using the 2016 version of the Merrill Reasers and Skills Books, the page numbers may be off by one page.

• Next you will do a dictation. (Erase your board!)

> Dictate *tap* and ask the children how they would change the word to *tape.*
>
> Dictate *hat* and have the children change it to *hate.*
>
> Dictate *plan* and have the children change it to *plane.*

• Dictate five or six more words and two sentences from the lists below.

same	make	take	came
made	gave	save	game
late	cake	hate	plane
bake	safe	care	brave

> A hero is someone who is very brave.
>
> Did the game start late?
>
> Jane's sister made a quilt and gave it to me.
>
> Jane and Dave take the same bus.
>
> Dave came over and helped us make cupcakes.
>
> Was your plane late?

The procedure for reviewing phonograms changes in Book F. From now on, you will only use review cards for a visual review, showing the children the cards as a prompt. You will not use the cards for the auditory review. Instead you will ask the children to write alternate spellings for sounds on their paper.

This is how you review long *a*:

Children respond to a visual prompt (letters)

Show the phonogram card to the children. Have them respond in unison by saying its sound, /ā/, and skywriting *a,* dash, *e* simultaneously.

Children respond to auditory prompt (sound)

Say, *Write two ways to spell /ā/.* The children respond by saying the sound and writing *a* and *a-e* on their papers in either order.

LEVEL 131	Stepping Up	Reader	Skills Book
Silent *e* Rule	70-72	8-10	5-6

The Silent *e* Rule explains how and when to change the spelling of a root word ending in silent *e* when adding a suffix. At this level, the students practice the rule using *a-e* root words.

Here's the rule:

In words ending with silent *e,* drop the *e* before a vowel suffix (care + ing = caring).

Do not drop the *e* before a consonant suffix (care + ful = careful).

Not all silent *e*'s are magic *e*'s that make the vowel long. For example:

> have + ing = having
>
> give + ing = giving
>
> come + ing = coming

Here's what you should do:

• Help the children figure out the Silent *e* Rule by having them compare what happens to a silent *e* when you add vowel suffixes and consonant suffixes to the same root words.

car*e* + ing = caring	care + ful = careful
shap*e* + ed = shaped	shape + less = shapeless
tast*e* + ing = tasting	taste + less = tasteless
wast*e* + ed = wasted	waste + ful = wasteful

• Download and use this form for the dictation. Remind the children that when they add a suffix to a root word that ends with silent *e*, they should ask themselves: *Is this a vowel suffix?* If the answer is yes, drop the *e*.

• Dictate *making. (Making: Dad is making dinner tonight.)*

• Ask the children what the root word is, and have them write *make* in the first column.

• Ask them what the suffix is, and have them write *-ing* in the second column.

• Ask them if *-ing* is a vowel suffix. Since the answer is yes, tell them to cross out the *e* and write *making* in the last column.

• Dictate the following words using the same procedure: baker, careful, taking, hated, shaping, shapeless, safest, careless.

Name Mia

Does the root word end with a silent *e*?
Does the suffix begin with a vowel?

If both answers are YES, drop the *e* and add the suffix.

Root Word	Suffix	New Word	
mak*e*	ing	making	✔
bak*e*	er	baker	✔
care	ful	careful	✔
tak*e*	ing	taking	✔
hat*e*	ed	hated	✔
shap*e*	ing	shaping	✔
shape	less	shapeless	✔
sav*e*	ing	saving	✔
care	less	careless	✔
saf*e*	est	safest	✔

Reading words in which a magic *e* has been dropped can be challenging for some students. They may not realize that the vowel in the root word is still long, because the magic *e* is not there. For example, some students may read *making* as *mă king*, since there is no magic *e*. To help your students become used to reading words of this kind, you may need to provide extra practice rereading word and phrase lists in Stepping Up.

In a subsequent lesson, you will use the same form to dictate another ten words: safer, saved, careless, later, baking, taking, caring, making, careful, bravest. This time say the word and have the children fill in all three columns, applying the rule independently.

PAF The Silent *e* Rule will be learned over time. As you move through Book F, you will review the rule three more times, using *i-e*, *o-e*, and *u-e*. Use the dictation form for homework. Write in root words and suffixes and have the children complete the third column.

LEVEL 132

	Stepping Up	Reader	Skills Book
	73-74	11-16	7, 24

Red Words: *could, would, should*

As each of these red words is introduced, teach the corresponding *not* contraction, *couldn't, wouldn't,* and *shouldn't.* Review how *not* contractions are formed, by dropping the *o* and adding an apostrophe.

> I could try baking a cake.
> Could we take a later plane?
> Dave couldn't go on the school trip.
> Jane couldn't finish drinking her milk.
>
> Mom would go to the game if she could.
> Jane said that she would call her friend later.
> Wouldn't it be safer to cross at the corner?
> I wish you wouldn't be so careless with my games.
>
> Should you swim in a thunderstorm?
> We should save some cake for later.
> Kids shouldn't run in the hall.
> You shouldn't brag to your friends.

LEVEL 133

	Stepping Up	Reader	Skills Book
	75-76	17-20	8-12

i-e (nine)

Now you will teach the third spelling of the long *i* sound. Previously the children have learned to spell long *i* with an *i* as in *tiger* (an open syllable) and with a *y* as in *fly*. In this lesson, they will learn that *i-e* spells *i* as in *nine*. Download the Spelling Choice Chart for long *i* with the first three spellings visible.

Here is what you should do:
- Teach the next magic *e* pattern the same way you taught *a-e* at Level 130. Use the following list of words.

        rip
        pin
        rid
        quit
        spin

	i	
i	tiger
i-e	nine
y	fly

- Next you will do a dictation.

    Dictate *hid* and ask the children how they would change the word to *hide*.
    Dictate *fin* and have the children change it to *fine*.
    Dictate *dim* and have the children change it to *dime*.

• Dictate five or six more words and two sentences from the lists below.

five	mine	side	shine
like	time	bike	drive
dime	mile	wide	smile
nine	ride	hide	sometimes

What could Jane get for nine dimes?
Sometimes I like taking a drive by myself.
Should we hide Mike's gift inside my desk?
Mike couldn't finish the long bike ride.
What time is it?
I think that dime is mine.

Remember, the children will do the auditory review on paper, not with skywriting. Say: *Write three ways to spell /ī/.* They should respond by saying the sound and writing *i, y,* and *i-e* on their papers in any order.

When the children are able to spell *i-e* root words, review the Silent *e* Spelling Rule using the same form you downloaded at Level 131 and these words: driver, hiding, widest, biking, wiped, timeless, smiled, timer, liked, shining.

LEVEL 134

	Stepping Up	Reader	Skills Book
Nouns and Verbs	77-79	21-22	13-18

Teach the concept that words can be categorized by meaning. Tell children that a noun is a word that is used to name a person, place, or thing; a verb is a word that describes what someone or something is doing. (At this level, do not use verbs that express a state of being, such as *be.*)

Conclude the lesson with a divided dictation using these words: dime, mile, take, snake, tame, bake, game, cake, make, give, hide, lake, plate, wipe, grape.

Nouns	Verbs

LEVEL 135

	Stepping Up	Reader	Skills Book
wh- (whale)	80-81	23-28	20
			(omit 19)

Most Americans do not pronounce *wh* with its first dictionary pronunciation, /hw/. Therefore, few children can hear the difference between *wh* (as in *whine*) and *w* (as in *wine*). In order to follow American speech patterns, *wh* is presented as a second spelling of the /w/ sound, the *h* being silent. This is an acceptable pronunciation.

The most important words for the children to spell at this level are the five *wh* question words, *who, what, when, where,* and *why.* So far the children have learned *who, what,* and *where* as red words. In addition to learning the two new spelling words, *when* and *why,* you want to make sure the children understand what kind of information each question word is looking for.

Who questions ask about a person(s).
What questions ask about a thing(s).
When questions ask about time.
Where questions ask about a place.
Why questions ask for a reason.

Here's what you should do:

• Introduce the new phonogram with the keyword card, making sure the children understand that the *h* is silent.

• Tell the children that the lesson today will be about the five question words that begin with *wh*. Put up a chart and have the children create and answer questions orally using the question words.

• Cover the chart and ask the children to write the five question words. Remind them that they all begin with *wh*.

• Dictate the following sentences with the new question words:

> When is your bedtime?
> Why couldn't we drive to school?
> Why is Mike smiling?
> When will the game be over?

?
who
what
when
where
why

You will do the visual review by holding up the *wh* card and having the children say /w/ and skywrite the letters. There is no auditory review.

LEVEL 136

	Stepping Up	Reader	Skills Book
	82-83	29-34	21-25

Red Word: *their*
Homonyms: *their, there*

Homonyms, sometimes called homophones, are words that are pronounced the same but are different in meaning and spelling. Homonyms cause many spelling errors. You will introduce the concept of homonyms with the red word *their*. The children will have to think about the meaning of a homonym in order to choose the correct spelling.

Here's what you should do:

• Tell the children that they are going to learn a second way to spell the word /thair/ and it is a red word. Write *their* on the board and explain that when /thair/ is spelled t- h-e- i- r, it shows possession, that something belongs to them. Explain the meaning of homonyms.

• Write *dog* next to *their* and have a child read the phrase *their dog*. Ask what belongs to them. Tell the children that the word *their* is usually followed by a noun. At this introductory level, the sentences have been controlled so that *their* is always followed by a noun (*their dog*) and not an adjective (*their white dog*).

• Practice writing *their* using the usual procedures for teaching a red word.

Their mom is coming on a bike ride with us.
Their friend Jane rides a bike to school.
Should we help them make their lunch?
Why is their class still inside the bus?
The kids left their bikes inside their yard.
When can their dad drive us to the game?

Before using Stepping Up, introduce the third spelling of /thair/, *they're* on the board. At this level, the children are expected to read, but not spell, the contraction.

In the following lesson, the children have to choose between the two spellings, *their* and *there*.

Here's what you should do:
• Write *their* and review its meaning (belonging to them). Remind the children that the word after *their* will usually be a noun. Then write *there* on the board and review when it is used (before *is, are, was,* or *were*).

> their (noun)
> there (is, are, was, were)

• Dictate *there* and *their* in isolation, reminding the children to wait until you use the word in a sentence so they can choose the correct spelling. You can dictate the words three or four times each in a mixed-up order. Then dictate two sentences for the children to write.

> Their dad is driving us to school.
> There were five dimes left in their bank.
> There was a snake hiding in their tent!
> Their bikes are the same brand as mine.
> Dave is wiping their car to make it shine.
> There is no time for taking a walk.

You will begin using a set of yellow homonym cards that can be found in Review Pack II.

Here is how you review homonyms:
Children respond to visual prompt (word)
Show the homonym card to the children. Call on one child to read the word and use it in a sentence.

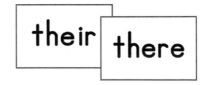

Children respond to auditory prompt (word meaning)
Say the word on an unexposed card and use it in a sentence. Have the children respond in unison by repeating the word and spelling it aloud, naming each letter as they skywrite. Show the class the homonym card.

LEVEL 137
o-e (bone)

	Stepping Up	Reader	Skills Book
	84-86	35-40	26-30

Now you will teach the second spelling of long *o*. So far the children have learned to spell long *o* with an *o* as in *go* (an open syllable). In this lesson, they will learn *o-e* as in *bone*. Download the Spelling Choice Chart for long *o* and display it with the first two spellings visible.

DOWNLOAD PAFprogram.com

Here is what you should do:
- Teach the next magic *e* pattern using the following list of words.

> hop
> rod
> not
> rob

o	
o	**robot**
o-e	**bone**

- Next you will do a dictation. (Erase your board!)

> Dictate *not* and ask the children how they would change the word to *note*.
> Dictate *hop* and have the children change it to *hope*.
> Dictate *rob* and have the children change it to *robe*.

- Dictate five or six more words and two sentences from the lists below.

home	vote	stove	close
rose	joke	smoke	those
bone	nose	chose	broke

> Why shouldn't you smoke?
> Their home is close to mine.
> Dave broke his nose when he fell off the bike.
> Did you vote yet?
> Are those bones on the stove for the dog?
> I chose those roses for my mom.

When the children are able to spell *o-e* root words, review the Silent *e* Spelling Rule using the same form you downloaded at Level 131 and these words: smoking, closest, hoping, hopeful, closer, homeless, voted, joking, closed, joker.

LEVEL 138
u-e (mule)
Red Word: *sure*

	Stepping Up	Reader	Skills Book
	87-90	41-46	31-36

Now you will teach the second spelling of long *u*. So far the children have learned to spell long *u*, with the letter *u* as in *music* (an open syllable). In this lesson they will learn *u-e* as in *mule*. Download the Spelling Choice Chart for long *u* and display it with both spellings visible.

Here is what you should do:
• Teach the next magic *e* pattern using the following list of words.

us
cub
cut

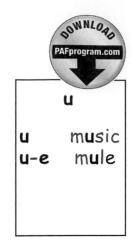

• Next you will do a dictation. (Erase your board!)
    Dictate *cub* and have the children change it to *cube.*
    Dictate *cut* and have the children change it to *cute.*
    Dictate *us* and have the children change it to *use* (s=/s/).

• Dictate the following sentences:

There is no use crying over spilled milk.
Do you think those tiger cubs are cute?
Don't use the stove until I get home.
Why is that shape called a cube?

When the children are able to spell *u-e* root words, review the Silent *e* Spelling Rule using the same form you downloaded at Level 131 and these words: useful, used, cuter, useless, using.

Red Word: *sure*

Those tiger cubs sure are cute.
Are you sure their pet is the cutest one?
Be sure the stove is off when you finish using it.
Their van sure uses a lot of gas.
Be sure to use a timer when baking.
I am sure Mike used their printer.

LEVEL 139
e-e (these)
Red Word: *because*

	Stepping Up	Reader	Skills Book
	91-93	47-52	37-41

Now you will teach the last of the magic *e* patterns, *e-e* as in *these*. The *e-e* spelling is usually found as the last syllable in two-syllable words such as *complete,* and not in one-syllable words. There are only two common one-syllable words that contain *e-e*, *here,* and *these*.

Download the Spelling Choice Chart for long *e* and display it with the first two spellings visible.

Here's what you should do:
• Review with the children what a magic *e* does to a vowel.

• Dictate *here* and *these* and three or four sentences.

> Come here!
> Are you sure these boxes will fit over here?
> The class uses these math cubes.
> Be sure you plant these roses here.
> Sit here and help me mark these papers.

Red Word: *because*

Tell the children that *because* is a word that is often used to answer *why* questions.

> Pete is here because his mom made him come.
> We chose these pups because they are cute.
> They are full because they ate all the cake!
> Pete was mad at Jane because she was late.
> Take these games home because we can't use them.
> We walked fast because we didn't want to be late.

LEVEL 140	Stepping Up	Reader	Skills Book
Silent *e* Syllables	94-99	53-58	42-46

You will now teach your students the fourth syllable type, silent *e* syllables. A silent *e* syllable ends with a vowel and consonant followed by an *e* (-tate, -treme, -clude). These syllables are always found at the end of words. After teaching these silent *e* syllables, you will have your students practice reading them in two-syllable words (*rotate, include*). The critical concept for your students to learn at this level is that if the last letter of a final syllable is a magic *e*, the vowel will make its long sound. Because there are no important words for the children to learn to spell at this level, you will go directly to Stepping Up to practice reading the new syllable type.

With the introduction of silent *e* syllables, you will need to teach the children something new about syllable division for reading unfamiliar words. Explain that whenever they go on a vowel hunt, they should only underline vowels that make a sound, not silent letters. When they come to an *e* at the end of a word, they should put a slash through the letter rather than underline it.

> in/vite
> cos/tume
> con/fuse

Time to stop teaching and give Proficiency Test #8.

LEVEL 141

ai (rain)

	Stepping Up	Reader	Skills Book
	100	61-64	—

Now you will teach the third spelling of long *a, ai* as in *rain*. This is the first of six vowel teams the children will learn in which the first vowel is long (*does the talking*) and the second vowel is silent (*does the walking*). Add *ai* to your Spelling Choice Chart and review pack. For the auditory review, you will ask the children to write three ways to spell /ā/.

In this first dictation, you can tell the children that every time they hear the sound /ā/, it will be spelled with an *ai*.

a		
a	baby	
a-e	snake	
ai	rain	

rain	nail	train	snail
pail	pain	paint	wait

The cars waited for the train to go by.
Jake has a painful cut because he fell.
What are you waiting for?
Jane used nails to hang the paintings.
The waiter handed us the menus.
Snails do not like to live where it is very hot.

In the following lesson, teach the *-air* words as a word family. The long *a* sound is distorted by the *r*.

air	hair	chair	airplane
pair	stairs	airport	

That pair of twins is a handful!
Who is taking Mike to the airport?
Jack put a pair of chairs in the van.
The pail of paint spilled on the stairs.
My friend waited for the barber to cut his hair.
I could use some fresh air after painting.

LEVEL 142

Spelling Choices: a-e/ai

	Stepping Up	Reader	Skills Book
	101	—	47-49
			(omit 50)

In this lesson, you will dictate words in which the long *a* sound is spelled either *a-e* or *ai,* in order to provide extra practice with common words. Children sometimes confuse these two spellings. The only way to make the choice is to remember the correct spelling for long *a*. Dictate these words: same, rain, wait, late, paint, take, gave, chair, game, air, train.

We had to wait for the train because it was late.
The game was called off because of the rain.
Who gave you a ride to the airport?
Put the painted chair in the fresh air to dry.
The printer you gave me is very useful.
Are you going to take the same train as I am?

LEVEL 143

	Stepping Up	Reader	Skills Book
Homonyms: ai/a-e	102	60, 65-70	51-52

You are going to introduce four sets of homonyms in this lesson.

Here's what you should do:

• Review the meaning of homonyms.

• Introduce *male* and *mail,* discussing the meaning of each word.

• Dictate *mail* and *male* two or three times each in a mixed-up order. Remind the children they have to wait until you use the word in a sentence to choose the correct spelling.

• Dictate one or two sentences with the new homonyms.

• Repeat this procedure with the remaining sets of words.

> **male-mail**
> Male spiders are smaller than females.
> The mail comes even when it is raining.
> Is their pet snake male or female?
> Jane painted the mailboxes.
>
> **sale-sail**
> What are you making for the bake sale?
> We couldn't go sailing because of the storm.
> Sails are like wings that make ships go.
> Jake got a pair of chairs at the yard sale.
>
> **tale-tail**
> Who is the hero of that tale?
> A tiger's tail is quite long.
> Planes have wings and a tail.
> Can you think of a tall tale?
>
> **plane-plain**
> Their plane landed late because of the rain.
> Jane put on a plain dress.
> Who invented the airplane?
> Plains are flat and have tall grasses.

Add these eight words to your homonym pack and shuffle the cards so the same homonyms do not follow each other.

LEVEL 144

-ay (gray)
Red Word: *says*

	Stepping Up	Reader	Skills Book
	103-104	–	53-55
			(omit 56)

This is another vowel team and the usual spelling of long *a* at the end of a one-syllable word. Children know four ways to spell long *a*: *a, a-e, ai,* and *ay*. Add *ay* to the Spelling Choice Chart and review pack.

day	pay	stay	today
may	May	play	Sunday
way	say	gray	Friday

To review, you will ask the children to write four ways to spell /ā/.

Jay can't play here today because he is still ill.
You should pay your bills on time.
May comes after April.
What day comes after Friday?
We stayed home Sunday and played games.
Maybe we can take a ride later.

Red Word: *says*

Jay says we should ask his sister to the play.
This chapter says that snails hate the sunshine.
Their friend says she will be here by twelve.
Ray's boss says she will pay him next Friday.
The menu says we can order snails!
Today's paper says it may rain Sunday.

LEVEL 145

ee (feet)
Red Word: *been*

	Stepping Up	Reader	Skills Book
	105-106	71-76	57-61

So far the children have learned two spellings of long *e, e* as in *begin* and *e-e* as in *these.* Now you will teach the vowel team *ee* as in *feet.* Add *ee* to your Spelling Choice Chart and review pack. To review, you will ask the children to write three ways to spell /ē/.

feet	deep	three	sweet
keep	feed	teeth	sleep
feel	need	tree	green

Keep off the grass!
There are three feet in one yard.
My mom says sweets can rot your teeth.
Kids need a lot of sleep to feel well.
Some trees stay green forever.
Is it safe to swim in the deepest part of the lake?

Red Word: *been*

Where have you been all day?
Have you ever been on an airplane?
What have you been feeding your pet snake?
The dentist asked if you have been brushing your teeth.
We have been hiking for over three miles.
They have been waiting in the driveway for today's mail.

LEVEL 146	Stepping Up	Reader	Skills Book
there (meaning *in that place*)	107-108	77-82	62, 64-66 (omit 63)

The children have been using *there* at the beginning of a sentence when it is followed by *is, are, was,* or *were.* Now you will teach another use of the word, when it means *in that place.* To help the children make the correct spelling choice, the word *there* always follows *over* in the dictated sentences. (Put that box over there.)

Put the glasses here and the plates over there.
Plant the trees over there by the lake.
They should put their paintings over there.
They need to keep their car parked over there.
Are you sure their mom is over there?
We shouldn't cross over there because it is not safe.

LEVEL 147	Stepping Up	Reader	Skills Book
ea (leaf)	109-110	83-88	67-72

Here is the fourth spelling for long *e,* the vowel team *ea.* Add *ea* to your Spelling Choice Chart and review pack. To review, have the children write four ways to spell /ē/.

eat	east	leave	dream
each	team	reach	beach
year	real	clean	teach

e	
e	me
e-e	these
ee	feet
ea	leaf

When is the longest day of the year?
Should we read the next chapter?
The sun comes up in the east and sets in the west.
Clean your hands and then we will eat.
Am I dreaming or is this real?
Make sure the beach is clean when you leave.

LEVEL 148

	Stepping Up	Reader	Skills Book
Spelling Choices: ee/ea	111	89-94	73, 75
			(omit 74)

In this lesson, you will dictate words in which the long *e* sound is spelled either *ee* or *ea* in order to provide extra practice with common words. These are the two long vowel spellings that are most frequently confused. The only way to make the choice is to remember the correct spelling for the long *e*. Dictate the following words: dream, sleep, tree, year, need, eat, keep, leave, feet, three, ear.

> My sister is over three feet tall.
> Do elm trees keep their leaves in the winter?
> Don't leave me here by myself.
> Do you dream when you are sleeping?
> I haven't been on an airplane in three years.
> We need to bring something to eat when we go sailing.

LEVEL 149

	Stepping Up	Reader	Skills Book
Homonyms: long *e*	112-113	95-100	71-81
Red Word: *does*			

You are going to introduce four sets of homonyms in this lesson using the same procedure you used at Level 143.

here-hear
You can hear Jay sing here later today.
Did you hear me say I was going to stay here?
I can hear the river when I stand over here.
Be sure to stay here until you hear the bell.

week-weak
Jane stayed home all week because she has been ill.
Even someone who is brave may sometimes feel weak.
Where have you been for three weeks?
She has been weak and taking naps all week.

see-sea
The sea is full of life.
You can see ships on the sea from over there.
Did you see the play last week?
Could you see the sea life from the side of the ship?

meet-meat
You should shake hands with someone you meet.
Do you like to eat meat?
Should you feed a dog meat all the time?
We will meet Jay here next week.

Red Word: *does*

Does the sun's heat make you feel weak?
Where does silver come from? (FYI: Rocks that are dug from mines.)
Does May come after April?
Doesn't your friend want to meet us next week?
Does this chair belong here?
Dave doesn't hear his mom calling him.

LEVEL 150	Stepping Up	Reader	Skills Book
oa (boat)	114-115	101-106	82-86

Homonyms: *road, rode*

Now you will teach the third spelling of long *o*. The children have learned *o* as in *robot* and *o-e* as in *bone*. In this lesson you will teach the first of two vowel teams that represent the long *o* sound, *oa* and *ow*. Add *oa* to the Spelling Choice Chart and review pack. To review, have the children write three ways to spell /ō/.

boat	oak	load	coast
soap	coat	toad	float

The land near the sea is called the coast.
The boat is loaded with boxes of soap.
Does the sailboat need a fresh coat of paint?
Toads have dry skin and short legs.
Oak trees shed their leaves in the fall.
There were three boats floating near the coast.

o	
o	robot
o-e	bone
oa	boat

Homonyms: *road, rode*

Joan rode her bike on the side of the road.
There were bumps in the road as we rode near the coast.
We rested on the side of the road after we rode up the hill.

LEVEL 151	Stepping Up	Reader	Skills Book
ow (snow)	116-117	107-112	87-88
			(omit 89)

The fourth and final common spelling of long *o* is the vowel team *ow* as in *snow*. It is the usual spelling of long *o* at the end of a one-syllable word. The *w* is actually a silent vowel in this phonogram. Add *ow* to the Spelling Choice Chart. To review, have the children write four ways to spell /ō/.

low	show	slow	grow
row	blow	snow	throw

o	
o	robot
o-e	bone
oa	boat
ow	snow

Be careful when driving in the snow.
What do you want to be when you grow up?
Throw the ball over here.
The river is low because it hasn't rained in weeks.
We lined the chairs up in rows for the show.
We will clean up the leaves after the wind stops blowing.

LEVEL 152	Stepping Up	Reader	Skills Book
Vowel Team Syllables	118-119	113-116	90-92

You will now teach your students the fifth syllable type, vowel team syllables. A vowel team syllable contains two vowels together that make one sound (-tain, rea-, -dow). The critical concept for your students to learn is to underline the two vowels as a unit and divide the word as usual. The vowel team will always make its regular sound. Because there are no important words for the children to spell at this level, you will go directly to Stepping Up to practice reading the new syllable type (*contain, reason, window*).

LEVEL 153	Stepping Up	Reader	Skills Book
-ck	120	–	95-96

You have already taught the children to double the letters *l, f,* and *s* after a short vowel (*bell, stuff, kiss*) in one-syllable words because **the short vowel needs an extra letter.** At this level, you will teach another example of this short vowel pattern, using *-ck* to spell /k/ at the end of one-syllable words (*back, stick*) instead of using *k* (*bake, shark*). The short vowel needs the extra letter *c*.

Here's what you should do:
• Use the following sets of words to help the children figure out that when you hear /k/ after a short vowel, you spell the sound *-ck*. Remind them that a short vowel often needs an extra letter to lean on.

rack	fake
deck	pork
pick	hike
sock	mark
tuck	week

• Next you will do a divided dictation in which the children have to choose between *-ck* and *-k.* Tell the children to ask themselves: *Do I hear a short vowel or not?* They do not have to identify the vowel sounds in the words, but they should simply decide whether the vowel is short or not short. Dictate these words: duck, check, oak, pack, take, quick, shark.

• Put the following words on the board.
> mask
> milk
> sink

- Ask, *What kind of vowel is in these words? Why do you think I did not use a* c*?* Help the children see that these short vowels already have an extra letter to lean on, the *s, l,* and *n.* They do not need the *c.*

- Continue the dictation with the following words: truck, trunk, sick, silk, blank, black.

In the next lesson, dictate the following words and two or three sentences: back, sick, shake, rock, ask, pork, luck, spoke, deck.

> Don't kick that rock because there is a toad under it!
> Do you think black cats are bad luck?
> Maybe those ducks are quacking because they need to eat.
> Pack the sleeping bags in the truck and lock it.
> Jack is using the deck of cards to show us tricks.
> Go check if you have a clean pair of socks.

LEVEL 154
-y as in *candy*

	Stepping Up	Reader	Skills Book
	121-122	117-118	93

The fifth and final common spelling of long *e* is the letter *y* as in *candy.* Teach the children that the sound /ē/ is spelled with the letter *y* at the end of words of more than one syllable. The *y* is doing the job of a vowel. Add *y* to the Spelling Choice Chart. To review, ask the children to write five ways to spell /ē/.

		e
e	begin	
e-e	these	
ee	feet	
ea	leaf	
y	candy	

candy	lady	tiny	body
party	story	copy	plenty
baby	ugly	pony	

> I need to copy over my story and fix the spelling.
> My class is going to throw a party next week.
> A baby needs plenty of milk to grow.
> The ugly bug had a black body and tiny legs.
> Jack says he will eat later because he just ate candy.
> The hero of the story saved the tiny baby.

You may want to have the children spell the months January and February, both of which end with the letter *y.* Help the children by saying the words for them syllable by syllable. Be sure to emphasize the first *r* in *February (Jan-u-a-ry, Feb-ru-a-ry).*

LEVEL 155
Adjectives
Suffix: -y
Red Word: *pretty*

	Stepping Up	Reader	Skills Book
	123-126	119-124	56, 76, 94

Beginning at this level, you will no longer use a Suffix Review Pack. New suffixes are simply added to the Suffix Chart and practiced by using them in dictations and reading them in Stepping Up.

Here's what you should do:

• Begin by reviewing nouns and verbs.

• Write these phrases on the board and have the children underline the nouns.

the green peas	a sweet drink
the slow train	the deep sea

• Circle the adjectives. Tell the children: *These words are neither nouns or verbs. They are describing words. They tell us something about the noun. These words are called adjectives and often come before a noun.* Write *adjective* on the board.

• Write these phrases and have the children think of appropriate adjectives for each noun:

my _____ coat	the _____ snake
a _____ tree	the _____ boat

• Write these phrases on the board:

a snowy day	the bumpy road
smelly sneakers	my messy desk

• Read the first phrase. Ask: *What is the noun? What is the adjective?* Underline the adjective. Continue this procedure with the three remaining phrases.

• Ask, *What is the same about all these adjectives?* (They end with the letter *y,* which makes the /ē/ sound.) Tell the children that the letter *y* is sometimes a suffix that changes a root word to an adjective. Add *y* to your Suffix Chart as a vowel suffix.

• Dictate the following phrases:

a windy day	a rainy week
those sleepy kids	a bumpy ride
snowy roads	sticky fingers

Red Word: *pretty*

The red word pretty is taught at this level because it is an adjective.

> There were lots of pretty songs in the show.
> We picked up some pretty plates for the party.
> That lady has on a pretty coat.
> We can picnic over there by the pretty trees.
> The story we are reading is pretty long.
> Making candy can be pretty messy.

LEVEL 156

Adverbs
Suffix: -ly
Red Word: *only*

	Stepping Up	Reader	Skills Book
	127-129	97-101	97-100

Here's what you should do:

- Begin by reviewing nouns, verbs, and adjectives. Tell them they are going to learn another kind of describing word.

- Write these phrases on the board and have the children underline the verbs.

> to run quickly
> to drive slowly
> to print neatly
> to speak softly
> to see clearly

- Circle the adverbs. Tell the children: *These words are another kind of describing word. They are called adverbs and often come after a verb.* Write *adverb* on the board.

- Ask, *What is the same about all these adverbs?* (They end with *-ly*.) Tell the children that the suffix -ly sometimes changes a root word to an adverb. Adverbs that end in -ly describe how something is done. Add -ly to your Suffix Chart.

- Dictate the following phrases:

> to read slowly
> to eat quickly
> to sit silently
> to copy neatly
> to think carefully

Red Word: *only*

There is only one day left until the party.
Be careful because that is my only copy of the story.
The tiny baby only has three teeth.
My friend can only visit me this Friday.
I think the smallest snake is only three inches long.

LEVEL 157

a as in *asleep*
Red Words: *again, against*

	Stepping Up	Reader	Skills Book
	130-131	125-130	101-105

Teach the children that when the letter *a* stands alone in a syllable, it usually says /ŭ/.

away	afraid	adult	awake
asleep	alive	agree	across
ago	alone	amaze	adopt

Is the baby awake or asleep?
Dave is only afraid of the dark when he is alone.
Jack agreed to go to camp for three weeks next year.
It is amazing that you finished cleaning up so quickly.
My teacher adopted a baby over five years ago.
Some baby snakes are born alive.

Red Words: *again, against*

Plenty of adults dream of being kids again.
Mr. and Mrs. Parker are trying to adopt a baby again.
The baby fell asleep again after she ate.
Are you for or against selling candy at school?
Nick was afraid when something banged against the window.
Don't lean against the wall again because the paint is wet.

LEVEL 158	Stepping Up	Reader	Skills Book
igh (light)	132-135	131-136	106-111

So far the children have learned three ways to spell long *i, i* as in *tiger, i-e* as in *nine,* and *y* as in *fly.* Now they will learn the fourth and last common spelling, *igh* as in *light.* Tell the children that in a one-syllable word when they hear long *i* followed by /t/, they will use *igh.* (FYI: There are four exceptions to this pattern: *bite, kite, white,* and *quite,* which you may choose to teach in a separate lesson.) Add *igh* to the Spelling Choice Chart and review by asking the children to write four ways to spell /ī/.

	i
i	tiger
i-e	nine
y	fly
igh	light

light	fight	bright	tonight
right	tight	lightning	midnight
night	might		

Dave likes to sleep with a small light on at night.
What is the brightest star in the night sky? (FYI: Venus)
A fight might end when someone gives up.
Lightning going across the sky can be very pretty.
Is it all right to stay at the party until midnight?
Why might someone be afraid of lightning?

Time to stop teaching and give Proficiency Test #9.

Merrill Book G -*Take Flight*

Beginning with Book G, many of the stories in the Merrill Readers are followed by nonfiction selections that deal with related topics. For example, a story in which a character reminisces about an experience trying to catch frogs is followed by a nonfiction piece about frogs and toads. As your students begin reading nonfiction, you will need to introduce them to new strategies that have been shown to improve comprehension, such as underlining important facts and taking notes. The most effective way to teach these strategies is to stop after each paragraph in the text to model what you are thinking as you read. In essence, you are thinking aloud. Show the children how you decide which ideas are important enough to underline and annotate.

In order to demonstrate how to mark up the text while reading, project a copy onto an overhead projector or interactive whiteboard. Also, make copies of the selection for your students in advance so they can mark their text as you mark yours. Underlining and note-taking are high-level comprehension skills that will take time for the children to learn. The goal in PAF is to introduce these skills and offer repeated opportunities to practice them under the guidance of a teacher.

If you are starting Book G in third grade, you should begin to teach cursive at this time. Display the Cursive Alphabet Wall Strip in your classroom, and follow the instructions for teaching cursive that are in the Appendix.

Throughout Books G and H, you will need to continue teaching homonyms. Homonyms, however, will no longer be listed in the instructional sequence. Instead, you should examine the original writing of your students to determine which homonyms they are misspelling and therefore need to be taught. Use the same procedures for teaching homonyms that you used in Book F, but you will need to create your own set of cards for review. Be sure your review pack contains no more than five or six pairs of homonyms at a time.

Finally, phonograms are no longer reviewed in isolation using the Review Pack cards. The only review sets you will use are the homonyms, discussed above, and the red words in Review Pack II. The children will write the red words on paper when doing the auditory review of red words, but they will still use skywriting for the visual review and for the introduction of red words.

**If you are using the 2016 verion of the Merrill Readers, visit PAFprogram.com
and click on *Free Downloads* for a schedule of page changes.**

LEVEL 159	Stepping Up	Reader	Skills Book
-en as in *kitchen*	1-3	5-9	1
(for reading only)			(omit 2)

You will find two word lists for *-en* in Stepping Up. On page 1, the -en is the second syllable of a root word. On page 2, *-en* is a suffix.

LEVEL 160	Stepping Up	Reader	Skills Book
Red Words: *woman, women*	4-5	10-12	3-6

Help children distinguish between the singular *woman* and the plural *women* by having them listen carefully to the difference in pronunciation.

> Seven women came to the party last night.
> The woman stared as the lightning struck the tree.
> Those women might go away the next weekend.
> The woman drove slowly because it was a snowy night.
> Are the women meeting again next week?
> Do you think that woman is friendly?

LEVEL 161	Stepping Up	Reader	Skills Book
-et as in *basket*	6-7	13-18	7-12

basket	pocket	planet	ticket
rocket	magnet	jacket	blanket

> Has a rocket ever reached the planet Mars?
> The women lined up to get tickets for the show.
> Planets orbit the sun.
> Would you put the picnic basket on the blanket?
> Some magnets are so big they can pick up a truck.
> The woman lost her jacket again.

LEVEL 162	Stepping Up	Reader	Skills Book
Doubling Rule	8-10	19-22	13-15

Sometimes the spelling of a root word changes when you add a suffix. So far the children have learned one rule for adding suffixes to root words, the Silent *e* Rule. Now you will teach them the Doubling Rule, which explains how and when to change the spelling of a one-syllable root word ending in a single consonant.

Here's the rule:
In one-syllable words ending with one consonant preceded by one vowel, double the consonant when adding a vowel suffix (ship + ing = shipping). Do not double the consonant when adding a consonant suffix (ship + ment = shipment).

There are no exceptions to this rule, though some words require an explanation for why the final consonant is not doubled. For example, a final *x* is never doubled because it represents two consonant sounds, /ks/, not one (fixing). The letters *w* and *y* are never doubled because they are vowels in the final position, not consonants (snowing, played).

Here's what you should do:
• Teach the children the following trick for knowing when to double.

Put your finger on the first vowel and count. If there are only two letters before the vowel suffix, double the final consonant.

1, 2 - Doubling I do!

ru̅b̅ + ing = rubbing   su̅n̅ + y = sunny

1, 2, 3 - No doubling for me!

cle̅a̅n̅ + er = cleaner   ra̅i̅n̅ + ed = rained

Download and use this form for the dictation.
• Dictate *dropped*. (*Dropped: I dropped the plate and broke it.*)

• Ask the children what the root word is, and have them write *drop* in the first column.

• Ask them what the suffix is and have them write *-ed* in the second column.

• Ask them if *-ed* is a vowel suffix. Since the answer is yes, tell them to put their pencils under the first vowel in the root word and count. Remind them of the rhyme: One, two, doubling I do.

• Dictate the following words using the same procedure: biggest, gladly, funny, chopping, runner, maddest, soapy, rubbed, spotless.

Name Olivia

Does the suffix begin with a vowel?
Does the root word end with a consonant?

Put your pencil on the first vowel and count.
1, 2 – Doubling I do!

Root Word	Suffix	New Word
drop	ed	dropped ✓
big	est	biggest ✓
glad	ly	gladly ✓
fun	y	funny ✓
chop	ing	chopping ✓
run	er	runner ✓
mad	est	maddest ✓
soap	y	soapy ✓
rub	ed	rubbed ✓
spot	less	spotless ✓

In the next lesson, you will use the same form to dictate another ten words: hitting, bigger, sadly, foggy, weakest, stopped, sunny, faster, stepping, running. This time just dictate the word and have the children fill in all three columns independently.

PAF The Doubling Rule will be learned over time. Reinforce it throughout Book G using the dictation form for homework. Write in root words and suffixes and have the children complete the third column.

LEVEL 163

-ore (store)

	Stepping Up	Reader	Skills Book
	11-12	23-28	16-19

The usual spelling of /or/ at the end of a word is *-ore.*

more	score	snore	wore
store	shore	chore	before

April comes after March and before May.
Long ago women wore long dresses.
The last batter scored the winning run.
I have to finish my chores before I can play basketball.
Lots of women were running along the shore this morning.
Does the store open before ten?

LEVEL 164

c as in *ice*

	Stepping Up	Reader	Skills Book
	13-15	29-33	20-22

The critical concept to learn at this level is that the letter *c* will say /s/ when followed by an *e, i,* or *y.* Reading words with soft *c* can be more difficult than spelling the words because the children have been saying /k/ for years. It takes practice for them to learn to look at the letter after a *c* in order to determine its sound.

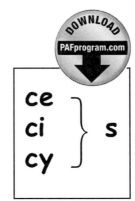

Here's what you should do:
• Write these words on the board:
> trace
> pencil
> fancy

• Read each word and ask the children what sound the *c* is making.

• Display the soft *c* chart and tell the children that when the letter *c* is followed by an *e, i,* or *y,* the *c* will say /s/.

• Read the word list in Stepping Up before giving a spelling dictation. The children must look at the vowel after each *c* and decide whether the *c* says /k/ or /s/.

• Next you will do a spelling dictation. There are no rules for when to use a *c* to represent the /s/ sound and when to use the letter *s.* The only way to know when to use a soft *c* instead of an *s* is to remember the spelling through practice.

• Dictate *ace.* Say: *Now you will spell some words that rhyme with* ace*.* Dictate these words: face, race, place, space.

• Dictate *ice.* Say: *Now you will spell some words that rhyme with* ice*.* Dictate these words: mice, rice, twice.

• Dictate the words *city* and *center*.

• Dictate two sentences.

> Some ice cream stores close in the winter.
> The price of this bag of rice is twice what it should be.
> There is a nice ice cream store in the center of the city.
> Did the runners quit the race because the track was muddy?
> The space center has some of the biggest rockets ever made.
> The seashore is a nice place to go jogging.

LEVEL 165	Stepping Up	Reader	Skills Book
-ce as in *dance*	16-19	34-36	23-25
Red Word: *once*			

The *e* at the end of these words keeps the *c* soft but does not affect the vowel sound.

dance	peace	since	chance

> The tiny baby had a peaceful night's sleep.
> That store is much nicer since it is in a bigger space.
> Should we take a chance and enter the dance contest?
> I didn't get a chance to eat before shopping.
> The kids stopped fighting and made peace.

Red Word: *once*

> Do you feed your pet mice once or twice a day?
> My feet felt fine once I stopped jogging.
> Lightning once struck a tree in the center of the city.
> I once had a dream that I was lost in space.
> Once upon a time there was a queen who was very lonely.
> You can go to the dance once you finish your chores.

LEVEL 166	Stepping Up	Reader	Skills Book
Syllable Division: VCCCV	20-22	37-44	26, 28-31
Red Word: *laugh*			(omit 27)

You will now teach the children how to divide unfamiliar multisyllable words that contain the following sequence of letters: one vowel, followed by three consonants, followed by another vowel (VCCCV). For example: **compl**ete, **hundr**ed. Words that follow the VCCCV pattern are usually divided after the first consonant (com/plete), unless dividing that way does not produce a word. In that case, the word is divided after the second consonant (emp/ty). Dividing after the first consonant will work in the vast majority of words.

Here's what you should do:
- Write the following words on the board.

    complete   explain

    hundred   monster

- Tell the children to go on a vowel hunt (underlining the sounded vowels).

    compl<u>e</u>t<u>e</u>   <u>e</u>xpl<u>ai</u>n

    h<u>u</u>ndr<u>e</u>d   m<u>o</u>nst<u>e</u>r

- Ask, *What will we do with three consonants, not two, between the vowels?* Tell the children they should always start by dividing after the first consonant because most words fit this pattern.

    com/plete   ex/plain

    hun/dred   mon/ster

- Sometimes dividing after the first consonant does not produce a word (em/pty, par/tner). In these cases, tell the children to move over one letter and divide after the second consonant. Have them try to read the word again (emp/ty, part/ner). This division produces a word.

Have the students practice VCCCV syllable division using the words in Stepping Up.

Red Word: *laugh*

It isn't nice to laugh when someone makes a mistake.

My best friend laughs at all my jokes.

The show was so funny the woman couldn't stop laughing.

The kids might not feel like laughing when their mom gets home.

I once laughed so hard that I started crying.

The kids began to laugh when the woman made a funny face.

# **LEVEL 167**	Stepping Up	Reader	Skills Book
Special Syllable Endings: -ble, -fle, -gle, -kle	23-25	45-52	32-38

You will now teach the sixth, and last, syllable type, special syllable endings. Special syllable endings contain a consonant followed by the letters *le* as in *table* and *giggle,* and they are always treated as a three-letter unit. They are special because they are the only syllables without vowel sounds.

The critical concept for reading is to take off the special syllable ending in order to determine the vowel sound in the preceding syllable. Do not put a slash through the silent *e*.

Here's what you should do:
- Write the following words on the board, with the last three letters in color.

bub**ble**	gig**gle**	sni**ffle**	fre**ckle**
bi**ble**	bu**gle**	ru**ffle**	spar**kle**
mar**ble**	jun**gle**	ri**fle**	twin**kle**

- Tell the children that they are going to learn about the last kind of syllable, a special syllable ending, and explain why it is special. Then tell them that a special syllable ending is made of three letters: a consonant followed by the letters _le. When they see this pattern at the end of a word, they should lop off the last three letters.

- Demonstrate how to remove the last three letters from the words, determine the vowel sound in the first syllable, and read each word.

bub(**ble**	gi**ggle**	sni**ffle**	fre**ckle**
bi(**ble**	bu**gle**	ru**ffle**	spar**kle**
mar(**ble**	jun**gle**	ri**fle**	twin**kle**

- Practice reading special syllable ending words in Stepping Up.

In a follow-up lesson, you will teach the children when to double the consonant to spell special syllable ending words. The critical concept for spelling is to double the first consonant in a special syllable ending after a short vowel (bubble, puddle). If the short vowel already has a consonant to lean on, you do not need to double the consonant in the special syllable ending (rumble, handle). This is another example of the short vowel needing an extra letter.

Here's what you should do:
- Tell the children: *Spelling words with special syllable endings can be tricky. Suppose I wanted to spell the word* giggle. *What is the first syllable?* (/gĭ/). Write *gi* on the board. Ask, *What special syllable ending do you hear?* (/gl/) Leave a space after *gi* and write *-gle.* (gi gle)

- *Let's read what we wrote.* Cover the *-gle* and say *gīgle. But the word is* giggle. *What could we do to make the* i *say /ĭ/ in the first syllable? How could we make that vowel short?* Teach the children that when they hear a short vowel followed by a special syllable ending, they must double the first consonant in the special syllable ending.

- Dictate these words: giggle, bubble, marble, table, pebble, fable.

- Tell the children: *Suppose I wanted to spell the word* tumble. *What is the first syllable?* (/tŭm/) Write *tum* on the board. *What special syllable ending do you hear?* (/bl/) Leave a space after *tum* and write *-ble.* (tum ble)

- *Let's read what we wrote.* Cover the *-ble* and say *tumble. What kind of vowel do you hear in the first syllable?* (short) *Why don't we have to double the* b? Teach the children that if the short vowel in the first syllable already has a letter to lean on, you do not have to double the consonant.

- Dictate these words: single, angle, juggle, able, jungle, dribble.

- Dictate one or two sentences.

> Not a single student is able to juggle.
> What is the name of a fable set in the jungle? (FYI: The Lion and the Mouse)
> All the angles in a square are right angles.
> I laughed when the bubble popped all over my face.
> Place those baskets over there under the table.
> A marble is a glass ball used in games.

LEVEL 168
Special Syllable Endings:
-dle, -ple, -tle, -zle
Red Word: *people*

	Stepping Up	Reader	Skills Book
	26-29	53-56	39-41

riddle	apple	little	title
maple	candle	drizzle	middle
bottle	puzzle	simple	puddle

What would be a funny title for that fable?
The kids laughed as they stepped in the muddy puddle.
Did that simple riddle puzzle you?
Is there a simple way to get sap from a maple tree?
Put a little more milk in the bottle.
Place the candles in the middle of the table.

Red Word: *people*

The people giggled at his funny riddles.
All people who have the right to vote should use that right.
The store was full of people shopping for gifts.
They closed the middle school today so people could vote.
Over a hundred years ago people still used candles for light.
People are able to visit more places since the car was invented.

LEVEL 169
g as in *magic*
(for reading only)

	Stepping Up	Reader	Skills Book
	30-32	57-62	42-44

The letter *g* usually says /j/ before *e, i,* or *y* (soft *g*). Display a soft *g* chart. The children will need practice looking at the letter after a *g* to determine whether the *g* makes a /g/ or /j/ sound.

ge
gi } j
gy

LEVEL 170
-dge
Red Words: *build, built*

	Stepping Up	Reader	Skills Book
	33-34	63-68	45-49

Now you will teach another example of a short vowel needing an extra letter. The sound /j/ is spelled *-ge* or *-dge* at the end of one-syllable words (large, bridge). The short vowel needs the extra letter *d*. There are a few short vowel words that already have an extra letter to lean on (bulge, fringe), but they are uncommon and not practiced for spelling.

Here's what you should do:
- Write the following sets of words on the board, with the vowels in color.

badge	page
edge	large
ridge	huge
lodge	charge
budge	strange

- Tell the children: *Today you are going to learn how to spell /j/ at the end of a word. No words in English end with the letter* j. *When you hear /j/ at the end of a word, you will spell it* -ge *or* -dge. Write *-ge* and *-dge* on the board over the appropriate words.

- *Listen to the vowel sound in these words.* Read the first list aloud. Ask: *What kind of vowels are in these words?* (short vowels) *How did I spell the /j/ sound?* (-dge)

- *Now listen to the vowel sounds in these words.* Read the second list aloud. Ask: *Are these short vowels?* (no) *How did I spell the /j/ sound?* (-ge)

- *Who can tell me when I added the* d? (after the short vowel)

- Help the children formulate the rule that when you hear /j/ after a short vowel, you spell the sound *-dge*. Remind them: *A short vowel often needs an extra letter.*

- Next you will do a divided dictation in which the children have to choose between *-dge* and *-ge*. Remind the children to ask themselves: *Do I hear a short vowel OR NOT?* They do not have to identify the vowel sounds in the words. They must simply decide whether the vowel is short or not. Dictate these words: page, edge, judge, age, bridge, change, fudge, huge, large, strange, cage, ledge.

-dge	-ge

In the next lesson, dictate three or four of the following sentences:

Fudge is made on large marble tables.
I keep extra change in my car for crossing bridges.
There was a strange woman walking across the bridge.
Who put those large bottles on the window ledge?
The judge made the driver pay a huge fine.
The land at the edge of a large river is called the shore.

Red Words: *build, built*

Someday I would like to build huge bridges.
Jogging helps people build strong bones.
The people who live in this building are very friendly.
The Empire State Building was built in 1931.
The campers built a fire near the edge of the river.
Some beavers built a dam in the middle of the pond.

LEVEL 171

Twin Consonants
(for spelling only)

	Stepping Up	Reader	Skills Book
	35	69-76	50-56

These words follow the VCCV pattern that the children have been reading since Level 81. They are taught as a separate level for spelling because children have to learn to double the middle consonant. This is another example of the short vowel (in the first syllable) that needs an extra letter.

The words in the last column contain short vowels in the second syllable that do not make their regular sound. (FYI: Vowels in unaccented syllables usually make the short u sound called a schwa /ə/ sound.) Dictate these words by saying them first as spoken (gallən), and then resaying them with an emphasis on the last vowel sound (gallŏn).

better	rabbit	follow	gallon
happy	yellow	silly	bottom
summer	ladder	address	kitten
dinner	penny	letter	sudden

We need a ladder to get the silly kitten off the ledge.
We were happy for the chance to rest before dinner.
Could we change seats so I can see the stage better?
Some rabbits build nests.
The gallon of milk started leaking from the bottom.
All of a sudden the cars stopped in the middle of the bridge.

You will find a sample lesson for this level on pages 205 to 207.

LEVEL 172

-age as in *cabbage*

	Stepping Up	Reader	Skills Book
	36-37	77-82	57-62

village	package	luggage	bandage
message	garbage		

A fable is a story with a message.
They packed extra luggage for their summer trip.
Will you address the package and send it right away?
People build villages on the edge of rivers.
The garbage is only picked up once a week.
The runner has to bandage her leg before the race.

Time to stop teaching and give Proficiency Test #10.

LEVEL 173

	Stepping Up	Reader	Skills Book
	38	83-85	63-66

-ild as in *child*
-ind as in *kind*

An *i* is frequently long before two consonants. Many years ago, most of these words actually had a silent *e* that made the vowel long (childe).

child	wild	mild	find
kind	mind	blind	behind

Wasn't it strange that the winter was so mild?
What kind of bridges might you find in a city?
Did you find the child who was hiding behind the building?
It was kind of the child to help the blind man cross the street.
Is it all right if I change my mind and stay behind tonight?
Name three kinds of cats that live in the wild. (FYI: Cheetahs, lions, leopards, and tigers live in the jungle.)

LEVEL 174

	Stepping Up	Reader	Skills Book
	39-40	86-90	67-68

-old as in *cold*
-ost as in *most*
-olt as in *colt*

An *o* is frequently long before two consonants. These words also once had a silent *e* that made the vowel long (olde). The word *both* follows this long *o* pattern.

old	gold	cold	colt
hold	fold	most	both
told	sold	post	postage

Some people don't mind the cold winter.
Would you hold the bottom of the ladder in place for me?
People post lots of messages on their computers.
You could help set the table for dinner by folding the napkins.
My two oldest children are both in high school.
Most letters need a single postage stamp.

LEVEL 175

	Stepping Up	Reader	Skills Book
	41-42	91-98	69-75

er (fern)
Red Words: *any, many*

There are three common ways to spell the sound /er/: *er, ir,* and *ur.* The children will have to choose between these three spellings. Since Level 86, they have been using *er* to spell /er/ as a final sound. At this level, they will learn words in which /er/ is in the middle of a word or syllable.

germ	concert	perhaps	expert
serve	person	permit	

That kind person served the child a huge dinner.
Perhaps my mom will permit me to go to the rock concert.
That judge is the oldest person to ever serve in this state.
Someday I would like to be an expert in building bridges.
What kind of person would like to explore space?
Some kinds of germs are useful.

Red Words: *any, many*

Are there any messages for me?
Perhaps you should clean your hands to get rid of any germs.
Does anybody have tickets for tonight's rock concert?
I am the kind of person who could live anywhere.

Many people go back to school after they retire.
Many of my friends have their driving permits.
There are old villages built on the edges of many rivers.
Many people think lightning doesn't strike the same place twice.

LEVEL 176

wr- (wrist)

	Stepping Up	Reader	Skills Book
	43-44	99-102	76-78

write	wrap	wrong	wreck
wrote	wrist		

I think I wrote the wrong address on the package.
Be sure to throw any candy wrappers in the garbage.
Write a friendly letter to any person you like.
There are many large wrecks at the bottom of the sea.
Use a postcard if you are only writing a short message.
Is anything wrong with your wrist?

LEVEL 177

Multisyllable Root Words
(of three or more syllables)

	Stepping Up	Reader	Skills Book
	45	103-104	79-81

Until now the children have been spelling and reading two-syllable root words. Now you will practice spelling and reading root words of more than two syllables.

For the introductory lesson, you will dictate each word and then resay it syllable by syllable for the children. Use this form to help the children focus on each syllable as they spell. There are no new sounds in these words.

Here's what you should do:

• Tell the children that they are going to spell some long words that are easy to spell if they are broken down into syllables.

- Dictate these months: September (*Sep-tem-ber*), October (*Oc-to-ber*), November (*No-vem-ber*), December (*De-cem-ber*), January (*Jan-u-a-ry*).

- Dictate the word *February.* Be sure to emphasize the *r* in the second syllable (*Feb-ru-a-ry*).

- Next you will dictate some adjectives. *Every* and *different* have to be broken into three syllables for spelling, although they are normally pronounced in two syllables. Dictate these words interesting (*in-ter-es-ting*), important (*im-por-tănt*), every (*ev-er-y*).

- Three words contain twin consonants, and you have to be sure to pronounce the consonants two times. Dictate these words: difficult (*dif-fi-cult*), excellent (*ex-cel-lent*), different (*dif-fer-ent*).

- Now you will show the children how to divide and read multisyllable root words. Put the following words on the board.
    electric
    detective
    ornament

- Have the children underline the sounded vowels and divide each word into syllables. Make sure to stress that they will have to divide the word in more than one place, between the first and second vowel, and then between the second and third, etc.
    <u>e</u>/l<u>e</u>c/tr<u>i</u>c
    d<u>e</u>/t<u>e</u>c/t<u>i</u>ve
    <u>or</u>/n<u>a</u>/m<u>e</u>nt

In a subsequent lesson, you will include sentences in your dictation.

> Have you been anywhere interesting lately?
> Why is it important to edit your writing?
> January comes after December and before February.
> Everyone agreed that dinner was excellent.
> There are many different kinds of germs.
> Did you get anything wrong on that difficult test?

From now on you will find multisyllable words that have not appeared on previous levels included in sentences for dictation. These words will only contain sounds the children know and therefore can be sounded out, such as *family* and *president.*

LEVEL 178	Stepping Up	Reader	Skills Book
eigh (eight)	46-47	105-110	82-87, 93

> eight   weigh   weight

> Is eight times ten more than eighty?
> An octopus has eight arms and a spider has eight legs.
> What is the weight of that large package?
> Every baby gets weighed when it is born.
> Does a penny weigh more than a dime? (FYI: A penny weighs more.)

Before you read the lists in Stepping Up, put the words *holiday, president,* and *uniform* on the board. Use them to teach the children that *i* usually says /ĭ/ in the middle of a long word (three or more syllables).

LEVEL 179
ur (purple)

	Stepping Up	Reader	Skills Book
	48-49	111-113	88-91
			(omit 92)

Now you will teach the second spelling of /er/, *ur* as in *purple*. Display a Spelling Choice Chart with the first two phonograms visible. Ask the children to write two ways to spell /er/ as part of your daily review. Point out that the days of the week that have an /er/ sound are spelled with *ur*.

fur	burn	purple	Thursday
turn	church	surprise	Saturday
hurt	turtle		

Many people go to church on Saturday night.
It is important to remember to turn off the lights.
Their family is planning a surprise party next Thursday.
What kind of animal has fur? (FYI: A mammal)
A turtle is a kind of reptile.
Did anyone get hurt in the burning building?

LEVEL 180
kn- (knee)

	Stepping Up	Reader	Skills Book
	50-51	114-118	94

know	knot	knock	knife
known	knee		

Did you know there are many different kinds of knots?
It is important to knock before you enter.
Perhaps a computer expert will know what is wrong.
Did you find a knife so we can serve the cake?
That family has known me since I was eight years old.
It will be difficult to race Saturday because I hurt my knee.

LEVEL 181
ir (bird)

	Stepping Up	Reader	Skills Book
	52-53	119-124	95-100

Now you will teach the third common way to spell /er/, *ir* as in *bird*. Add *ir* to the Spelling Choice Chart. Begin to ask the children to write three ways to spell /er/ as part of the review. Point out that number words are spelled with *ir*.

girl	shirt	third	circus
bird	skirt	thirty	thirsty
dirt	first	thirteen	birthday

er	
er	fern
ur	purple
ir	bird

We will take the twins to the circus on their third birthday.
Did you know the smallest bird is a hummingbird?
Remember to take the dirty shirts and skirts to the cleaners.
That girl is thirteen years older than you are.
The first day of January is a holiday.
Running in the summer makes me really thirsty.

In a subsequent lesson, do a dictation in which the /er/ sound is spelled either *er, ur,* or *ir* in order to provide extra practice with common words. The only way to make the choice (except for the days of the week and number words) is to remember the correct spelling.

Dictate these words: girl, hurt, bird, turn, dirt, surprise, perhaps, birthday, purple, person, circus, yesterday.

Perhaps your family would like to go to the circus on Saturday.
I know a girl who will turn thirteen on the first of February.
Every Thursday I clean the bird's dirty cage.
What is the name of the person who wrote this excellent story?
Have you ever had your feelings hurt?
Everybody had fun at the surprise birthday party yesterday.

LEVEL 182	Stepping Up	Reader	Skills Book
ou (cloud)	54-55	125-132	101-107

This is the usual spelling of /ou/ at the beginning or middle of a word.

out	count	cloud	ground
loud	mouth	shout	around
found	south	round	thousand
pound	sound	proud	

The mouth of a river is where it meets the sea.
Many birds fly south in the winter.
An adult elk weighs about a thousand pounds.
It is important to know the different kinds of clouds.
Every night we hear loud sounds around the yard.
The little girl was proud she could count to ten without using her fingers.

The word *our* is often mispronounced as /ar/ and spelled incorrectly as *are.* Stress the /ou/ sound in the word *our* and dictate the following sentences.

The girls in our family are all excellent writers.
Are our friends coming to the surprise party?
All the plants around our school are different.

LEVEL 183

ow (brown)

	Stepping Up	Reader	Skills Book
	56-58	133-138	108-113

This is the usual spelling of /ou/ at the end of a word or syllable. The word *crowd* needs extra reinforcement because there is no explanation for using *ow* in the medial position.

now	how	flower	tower
cow	crowd	power	shower

The letters *ow* are often followed by an *n*.

down	brown	frown	crown
town	clown		

April showers bring May flowers.
There was a huge crowd of people shopping downtown.
A tower is a very high building.
The president is a powerful leader.
Some female animals are called cows. (FYI: Whales, bears and elephants)
How many clowns can fit in that little car?

Follow up with a dictation using sentences which contain both spellings of /ou/.

Our family is building a cabin down south.
Quit clowning around!
The crowd shouted as our president finished his speech.
Our child knows how to build towers out of blocks.
What is making that strange sound downstairs?
Some people never go out without taking a shower.

LEVEL 184

al- as in *almost*
Red Word: *together*

	Stepping Up	Reader	Skills Book
	59-60	139-143	116-120

These are actually compound words in which the first word, *all,* drops an *l*.

also	almost	always

Red Word: *together*

Almost a thousand people came together for the peace march.
My sister and I always go downtown together on Thursdays.
We raked the leaves together and also weeded the flower garden.
Friends should always stick together.
We almost have this difficult puzzle put together.
Our family almost always has dinner together on Saturday.

Tell the children the words on page 60 in Stepping Up are compound words and therefore do not follow the rules for syllable division.

LEVEL 185
w(or) as in *work*

	Stepping Up	Reader	Skills Book
	61-62	144-148	114-115

The sound /er/ is spelled *or* after the letter *w*.

work   worm   world   worst
word

Always back up the work you do on a computer.
Who was the first woman to fly around the world? (FYI: Jerrie Mock in 1964)
We almost always dig for worms before fishing.
We did our homework together and also finished the crossword puzzle.
We all went out together after the worst of the storm was over.
Everyone should always work for world peace.

LEVEL 186
w(ar) as in *warm*
Red Word: *water*

	Stepping Up	Reader	Skills Books
	63-65	149-153	121-127

The sound /or/ is spelled *ar* after the letter *w*. Since *qu* represents the sound /kw/, the sound /or/ is also spelled *ar* after the letters *qu*.

war   warn   quart   quarter
warm   award

How many pints are in a quart?
Flashing yellow lights serve as a warning to drivers.
Our sister is always home from work by a quarter after seven.
The firefighter was proud to be given an award.
How do you warm your home?
Everyone hopes for a world without wars.

Red Word: *water*

Did you know that water is a part of every living thing?
It is important to drink about eight glasses of water a day.
Swimming and diving are both water sports.
Water turns to ice when it gets very cold.
A waterfall is a stream of water that falls from a high place.
What is the world's tallest waterfall? (FYI: The tallest falls is Angel Falls in South America.)

Time to stop teaching and give Proficiency Test #11.

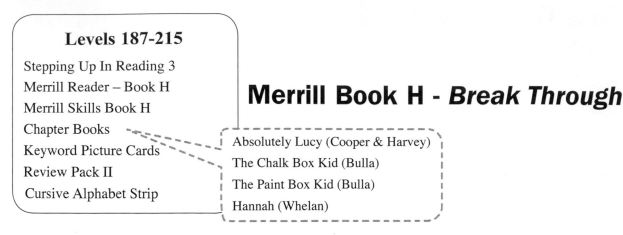

Levels 187-215

Stepping Up In Reading 3
Merrill Reader – Book H
Merrill Skills Book H
Chapter Books
Keyword Picture Cards
Review Pack II
Cursive Alphabet Strip

Merrill Book H - *Break Through*

Absolutely Lucy (Cooper & Harvey)
The Chalk Box Kid (Bulla)
The Paint Box Kid (Bulla)
Hannah (Whelan)

By the time you get to Book H, some of the children will still need the Merrill Readers, and they will continue in the sequence as it is written. Other children, those who can read text containing sounds you have not yet taught, will be ready to leave the controlled Readers for chapter books. In order to determine if children are ready to leave the Merrills, have them read the first page in the book *Hannah,* by Gloria Whelan. If they can read the page with fewer than six errors, they are ready for chapter books and can begin to read *Hannah* with you. Otherwise they should continue to read in Book H. All your students will read chapter books before they finish the instructional sequence.

Although the children may be reading different books, they will still do their dictations as a group and will all read Stepping Up in Reading and their books with you. The only change in routine should be that the children reading chapter books now do their Skills Books independently.

Once your students begin reading chapter books, you will need to use the same care in preparing and implementing reading comprehension lessons that you used with the Merrill Readers. Begin by prereading the chapter book. Decide what the book is about. What is the theme or main idea? What problems do the characters face, and how do they attempt to solve these problems? Does the book have a moral (for fiction) or does it teach new information (for nonfiction)? Be sure to ask yourself if there is any background information or vocabulary that is critical to understanding the book. Plan your lessons, chapter by chapter, using the same reading format—before, during, after—that you used in your prior comprehension lessons.

With chapter books, it is important to read at a pace that will keep the narrative moving along in order to sustain interest. Continue to have your students read aloud each day in class, and assign the next part of the story each night for homework. Reading homework should take approximately a half hour. As part of each reading assignment, send home one or two written questions for your students to answer. This will allow you to monitor if they are doing the reading and understanding the story. Begin each lesson with a discussion of what was read at home in order to address any comprehension issues. Have the students summarize what they have read and make logical predictions about what might happen in the next chapter.

**If you are using the 2016 verion of the Merrill Readers, visit PAFprogram.com
and click on *Free Downloads* for a schedule of page changes.**

LEVEL 187

	Stepping Up	Reader	Skills Book
-rr as in *arrow*	66-67	5-10	1-6

When a short vowel is followed by the sound /r/, the *r* is doubled (hurry, narrow). This is another example of the short vowel needing an extra letter. For reading, the children need to learn that when they divide a word between two *r's*, the first vowel will be short, not *r*-controlled.

carry	sorry	hurry	borrow
berry	marry	narrow	tomorrow

The flashing lights warned us to be careful of the narrow bridge.
Larry is going to marry Beth tomorrow.
Harry asked to borrow a quarter.
Larry was sorry he dropped the jar of blackberry jam.
Barry was in a hurry to finish his homework.
Always carry water and a flashlight when hiking.

LEVEL 188

	Stepping Up	Reader	Skills Book
o as in *love*	68-70	11-20	7-12
Red Word: *father*			

In the Middle Ages, scribes started using a style of calligraphy that made it difficult to distinguish the letter *u* when it was followed by *m*, *n*, or *v*. To improve legibility, the scribes replaced *u* with the letter *o*. The scribal *o*, which makes the sound /ŭ/, appears in the red words *of, from, one, done, none, once, some,* and *come.*

won	other	above	Monday
ton	month	mother	wonder
son	glove	brother	discover
love	dozen	nothing	another
front	cover		

May I borrow a dozen eggs?
My brother lives in the apartment above us.
Mondays are wonderful because I have nothing to do.
The skin is the outer covering of your body.
Barry's son won an award for discovering another star.
Is February the coldest month of the year?

Red Word: *father*

Your mother's father is your grandfather.
Both my father and my grandfather come from Mexico.
Our father wrote that story about the war.
Father's Day is the third Sunday in June.
What do you call your father's brother?
We love our wonderful stepfather.

LEVEL 189
ea (feather)

		Stepping Up	Reader	Skills Book
		71-72	21-26	13-19

read	dead	weather	ahead
head	heavy	feather	ready
bread	health	sweater	already

I read that it is healthy to exercise.
Heavy sweaters and gloves keep you warm in cold weather.
Does a ton of feathers weigh more than a ton of bricks?
Our teacher always walks ahead of the class.
Nothing smells as wonderful as freshly baked bread.
My father already put the heavy box on the front seat.

LEVEL 190
Y Rule
Red Word: *buy*

	Stepping Up	Reader	Skills Book
	73-75	27-38	20-25

So far the children have learned two rules for adding suffixes to root words: the Silent *e* Rule and the Doubling Rule. Now you will teach the *Y* Rule, which explains how and when to change the spelling of a root word ending in the letter *y*.

Here's the rule:
In words ending with the letter *y* preceded by a consonant, change the *y* to *i* and add the suffix **unless** the suffix begins with an *i* (cried, crying). For the first time, it does not matter whether the suffix begins with a vowel or a consonant.

Teach this lesson in two parts. First, teach the children the general rule that if there is a consonant before the *y*, they must change the *y* to an *i* and add the suffix. Then, after the children practice spelling words, show them the one exception: the *y* **does not** change if the suffix begins with an *i*.

Here's what you should do:
• Help the children figure out the *Y* Rule by having them look at the following words. Ask, *What happened to the* y *when I added the suffixes?*

try + ed = tried
fly + er = flier
carry + ed = carried

• Download and use this form for a dictation. Remind the children that if there is a consonant before the *y*, they change *y* to an *i* when adding a suffix. Dictate *hurried*. (*Hurried: We hurried to catch the train.*)

• Ask the children what the root word is and have them write *hurry* in the first column.

• Ask what the suffix is and have them write it in the second column.

• Ask the children if the letter before the *y* is a consonant. Since the answer is yes, tell them to change the y to an *i* and add the suffix.

Dictate the following words using the same procedure: happiest, player, dried, heavier, stayed, easily, worried, flier, laziest.

In a subsequent lesson, show the children that *y* preceded by a consonant does not change if the suffix begins with an *i,* using the following words:

cry + ed = cried   cry + ing = crying
fly + er = flier   fly + ing = flying

Then use the same form to dictate another ten words: tried, trying, drying, sprayed, carrying, carried, worrying, playful, hurrying, hurried.

Red Word: *buy*

I will buy dried flowers tomorrow.
You can buy almost anything online.
My mother tried to buy some fresh bread.
I hurried to buy a dozen eggs before they were sold out.
Father is buying me another sweater tomorrow.
Buy heavier gloves for the cold weather.

The Y Rule will be learned over time. Reinforce it throughout Book H using the dictation form for homework. Write in the root words and suffixes and have the children complete the third column.

LEVEL 191	Stepping Up	Reader	Skills Book
ea (steak)	76-77	39-44	26-31

great   break   steak

Teach the -*ear* words as a word family. The long *a* sound is distorted by the *r.*

bear   pear   wear   tear

Pears taste great!
I tried to buy dishes that wouldn't break easily.
Read this secret message and then tear it up.
The brown bear is the heaviest of all bears.
Our son has to wear a cast until the break mends.
Would you like steak or chicken for dinner?

LEVEL 192

	Stepping Up	Reader	Skills Book
ear (earth)	78-80	45-54	32-38

Do not capitalize the word *earth* after the word *the*.

earth	heard	early	earthquake
learn			

We learned that early man lived in caves.
Three quarters of the earth is covered by water.
Our son learned his spelling words because he studied hard.
The South Pole is the coldest place on Earth.
Have you ever heard of a bear named after a president? (FYI: Teddy bears are named after Theodore Roosevelt.)
It takes the earth one year to orbit the sun.

LEVEL 193

	Stepping Up	Reader	Skills Book
au (faucet)	81-82	55-62	39-44
(for reading only)			

This is the first of six vowel teams in which the first vowel is not long (*au, aw, oo, ie* as in *chief, oi* and *oy*).

LEVEL 194

	Stepping Up	Reader	Skills Book
aw (saw)	83-84	63-68	45-50

This is the usual spelling of /au/ at the end of a word or before an *n*.

saw	law	claw	lawn
paw	jaw	straw	dawn
raw	draw	yawn	fawn

Laws are made to keep people safe.
I will tear up that drawing and try again.
Bears have huge front paws and sharp claws.
Fawns are most active at dawn and dusk.
Some people yawn when they are bored or tired.
Lawns are always covered with grass.

LEVEL 195

	Stepping Up	Reader	Skills Book
oo (moon)	85-87	69-76	51-57

The common words *zoo, food,* and *room* have been omitted from the list since most children know them by this level. You can include them as spelling words, however, if you think the children need to practice them.

soon	noon	tool	smooth
moon	root	spoon	cartoon
pool	cool	tooth	afternoon

We will cool off in the pool this afternoon.
The same side of the moon always faces the earth.
A spoon is a kitchen tool for eating or serving food.
The oldest tools were most likely used for cutting and pounding.
Roots take in water and food for plants.
Ice has been discovered on the poles of the moon.

With the introduction of /oo/, you can teach the homonyms, *too, two,* and *to.* The word *too* means also (*please get me a sandwich too*), and it means extra (*this is too heavy for me to carry*) Check that the children can spell the red word *two.* The following sentences contain all three homonyms.

I am worried these two packages are too heavy to carry.
The weather is too cool to go to the pool.
Do your two brothers want to go to the zoo too?
My bedroom is too narrow for two beds.
My son lost his two front teeth too.
It is too soon to buy another computer.

LEVEL 196

	Stepping Up	Reader	Skills Book
Adding *s* to *y* words	88-90	77-82	58-63

This is an extension of the *Y* Spelling Rule. When adding the suffix s to words ending in *y* preceded by a consonant, change the *y* to an *i* and add *-es.* Dictate the root word and then have the children rewrite the word with the suffix -s (city/cities).

flies	pennies	babies	berries
tries	carries	hurries	families
stories	cities		

How many pennies are in a dozen dimes?
Name two cities near the Great Lakes.
Our father always hurries home after work.
Flies can carry germs.
My mother tries to take the babies out every afternoon.
Grandmothers love to tell stories about their families.

LEVEL 197

	Stepping Up	Reader	Skills Book
oo (book)	91-93	83-90	64-69

Red Word: *half*

In this list, the common words *good, look, took,* and *book* have been omitted since most children know them by this level.

foot	wood	hook	wool
cook	stood	hood	shook

Both friends shook hands and said they were sorry.
There are twelve inches in a foot.
The families on our block got together for a cookout.

A paw is the foot of an animal with claws.
I never understood why anyone would break the law.
A saw is a tool used for cutting wood.

Red Word: *half*

We have already read half the stories in our book.
Over half the buildings in the city are more than thirty stories high.
What is half of one dozen?
How many inches are there in half a foot?
How many pounds are in half a ton?
We ate half the berries that we picked in the woods.

LEVEL 198	Stepping Up	Reader	Skills Book
ie (chief)	94-96	91-96	70-76
ie (pie)			

The vowel team *ie* makes two sounds, /ē/ and /ī/. This is an uncommon spelling for these long vowels, and the children simply need to practice spelling these words. The first row contains words in which *ie* makes the sound /ē/. The second row contains words in which *ie* makes the sound /ī/.

piece	field	chief	believe
pie	lie	tie	die

Do you believe that white lies are wrong?
Tie up the pieces of wood so they are easier to carry.
Football fields are one hundred yards long.
One of the chief jobs of a rancher is to take care of cattle.
Everyone feels unhappy when their pets die.
Would you like berries or a piece of pie?

LEVEL 199	Stepping Up	Reader	Skills Book
oi (poison)	97	97-104	77-82

This is the usual spelling of /oi/ at the beginning or middle of a word or syllable.

oil	join	spoil	voice
soil	coin	point	choice

The cookbook says you have a choice between oil or butter.
Roots store food from the soil.
There is no point in everyone raising their voices.
More than half the coins in my bank are pennies.
Will that raw steak spoil if we leave it out too long?
Half the families on our block joined the town pool.

LEVEL 200	Stepping Up	Reader	Skills Book
oy (boy)	98-99	105-112	83-89

This is the usual spelling of /oi/ at the end of a word or syllable. The common words *boy* and *toy* have been omitted since most children know them by this level.

joy　　　　　　enjoy　　　　　　destroy　　　　　annoy

Did the girls and boys enjoy field day?
Earthquakes can destroy whole cities.
That toy is making an annoying sound!
Oil spills can destroy the earth.
We were annoyed that we lost by only one point.
We enjoyed the singer's wonderful voice.

Time to stop teaching and give Proficiency Test #12.

LEVEL 201	Stepping Up	Reader	Skills Book
aught as in *caught*	100	113-118	90-96
ought as in *bought*			
(for reading only)			

LEVEL 202	Stepping Up	Reader	Skills Book
Red Words: *rough, tough, enough*	101	119-128	97-104

Almost all the students finished the rough drafts for their stories.
Are you tough enough to stand up for what you believe?
These rough waters made it tough to sail safely.
Do you have enough coins for parking?
That's enough of being rough and tough!
Is there enough room to store the lawn mower?

LEVEL 203	Stepping Up	Reader	Skills Book
ue (blue)	102-103	129-134	105-111
Red Word: *Wednesday*			
Days of the Week			

This is the usual spelling of /ue/ at the middle or end of a word or syllable.

due	blue	Tuesday	rescue
true	clue	argue	avenue

An avenue is a wide street.
Our rough drafts are due next Tuesday.
It annoys me when you argue with your brother.
Don't believe that everything you read is true.
The firefighters were able to rescue everyone from the burning building.
The clues to this tough crossword puzzle are difficult.

Red Word: *Wednesday*

Teach the children to spell *Wednesday* by saying *Wed-nes-day* in order to hear all the sounds and syllables.

Wednesday comes after Tuesday and before Thursday.
I felt blue last Wednesday because field day was rained out.
Wednesday is the middle day of the week.
I hope enough children join our Wednesday afternoon book club.
Our report is due next Wednesday.
You have a choice of taking drawing on Tuesday or Wednesday.

Days of the Week

Children can now spell the names of the days of the week. Use the following types of cues for dictations to reinforce the sequence of the days.

Write the days of the week in order.
Write the day that comes after Monday.
Write the day that comes before Thursday.
Three days from today will be …

LEVEL 204

		Stepping Up	Reader	Skills Book
gu as in *guitar*		104	135-140	112-118

guess	guest	guard	guilty

The lifeguard rescued the swimmer from the rough waters.
My son felt guilty for telling me a lie.
My guess is we have enough pie for half the guests.
The beached whale was rescued by the coast guard.
Stop making wild guesses and think!
Do we have enough food for all our guests?

LEVEL 205
-tion as in *fraction*

	Stepping Up	Reader	Skills Book
	105-107	141-151	119-127

Words that end with *-tion* are nouns. This syllable is tricky to spell because *ti* represents the sound /sh/ and the /ŭ/ is written with a scribal *o*. When reading words that end with *-tion,* teach the children to take off the syllable and then divide as usual. The *i* before *-tion* will always say /ĭ/.

e̲/mo̲(tion
co̲n/di̲(tion

nation	station	pollution	direction
fiction	vacation		

Short stories are always fiction.
Nonfiction is about real people and true events.
Do you enjoy eating food that comes from other nations?
Can you point me in the direction of the train station?
Many families take summer vacations.
There are laws to try to prevent pollution.

Your students have finished the Merrill Readers and are ready for chapter books. The following three titles are an excellent transition to uncontrolled text: *Absolutely Lucy,* by Ilene Cooper and Amanda Harvey; and *The Chalk Box Kid,* and *The Paint Brush Kid,* both by Clyde Robert Bulla.

LEVEL 206
Silent Letters

	Stepping Up
	108-109

This level includes the special syllable ending *-stle*. Remember that *i* and *o* often make their long sound when followed by two consonants.

silent b	**silent h**	**silent t**
comb	hour	often
climb	honest	listen
thumb	ghost	castle

A castle is one of the pieces in a chess set.
Do you believe in ghosts?
How many hours are in a day?
It took the hikers hours to climb to the highest point.
You shouldn't feel guilty about an honest mistake.
My brother often enjoys listening to jazz.

LEVEL 207
ew (news)

Stepping Up
110-111

few	new	chew	newspaper

A few of my friends started a school newspaper.
Today's newspaper had a great story on pollution.
Many people enjoy going to New Year's Eve parties.
Chew your food slowly.
Which month has the fewest days?
Don't believe everything you read in the newspaper.

In a following lesson, present these irregular past-tense verbs.

grew (grow)	drew (draw)	threw (throw)
knew (know)	blew (blow)	flew (fly)

Guess who drew the cartoons for the school newspaper.
I already tied up and threw out the newspapers.
Many nations flew in food for the rescue workers.
The climbers knew which trails were the toughest.
Joy chewed her gum and blew bubbles until her jaw hurt.
A few of our plants grew huge.

LEVEL 208
ou (soup)
ui (fruit)
(for reading only)

Stepping Up
112-113

LEVEL 209
Months of the Year

Stepping Up
114-115

First, have the children spell *July*. Tell them that sometimes long *i* at the end of a multisyllable word is spelled with the letter *y*. Then, have them spell *August*. Children can now spell the names of all the months. Use the following types of cues for dictations in order to reinforce the sequence of the months.

Write the months in order.
Write the month that comes after July.
Write the month before August.
Three months from now is ...
Thanksgiving comes in ...

LEVEL 210

-sion as in *vision*
(for reading only)

Stepping Up
116-117

Words that end with *-sion* are nouns. This syllable makes two sounds, /shun/ as in *discussion* and /zhun/ as in *vision*. When reading words that end with *-sion*, take off the syllable and divide the word. The letter *i* before *-sion* will always say /ĭ/.

LEVEL 211

-sion as in *discussion*
(for reading only)

Stepping Up
118-119

LEVEL 212

-ain as in *mountain*

Stepping Up
120-121

mountain	certain	captain	fountain

What is the tallest mountain peak in the world? (FYI: Mt. Everest)
We learned that certain mountains are covered with snow all year.
The person in charge of a plane or ship is called the captain.
The Rocky Mountains are one of the chief mountain ranges in our nation.
Mountains are worn down by wind and ice.
I threw a few pennies into the fountain and made a wish.

LEVEL 213

-ture as in *picture*

Stepping Up
122-123

picture	future	nature	adventure

We certainly had a great adventure while mountain climbing.
I enjoy listening to stories that give a picture of the future.
Perhaps cities in the future will not have pollution.
Nature is everything in the world not made by people.
I believe that mountains are one of the greatest things in nature.
My son spends hours drawing pictures.

LEVEL 214

Red Words: *ocean, island*

Stepping Up
124-125

Atlantic Ocean   Pacific Ocean

The Pacific Ocean is larger than all the other oceans.
The tallest mountains are found underwater in oceans.
No light reaches the bottom of the ocean.
The Atlantic and Pacific Oceans border the United States.
Captain Cook was an explorer who sailed across the Pacific Ocean.
Certain parts of oceans are always covered with ice.

Most islands are found in oceans.
Some mountains rise out of the ocean to form islands.
Greenland is the largest island in the world.
Animals found on islands are often different from those in other places.
Certain islands are found in the middle of rivers and lakes.
An island is a piece of land completely surrounded by water.

LEVEL 215
ph (phone)
(for reading only)

Stepping Up
126-128

Words that contains the phonogram ph = /f/ are derived from the Greek language. (FYI: Also words that contains *y* = /ĭ/ as in gym or *ch* = /k/ as in school are from Greek.) The sequence ends by introducing two Greek roots: *phone* (meaning sound) and *graph* (meaning write). Use the last page in Stepping Up to show the children how learning the meaning of roots can help them understand the meaning of unfamiliar words. You may want to continue your spelling curriculum with a unit on common Greek and Latin roots.

Time to stop teaching and give Proficiency Test #13.

After completing the PAF instructional sequence, your students can continue to read and enjoy chapter books in a wide variety of genres. What follows are three lists of recommended titles. Each list represents a general level of difficulty. The books on each of the lists, however, can be taught in any order.

1   *Hannah* (Gloria Whelan)

      A Mouse Called Wolf (Dick King-Smith)

      The Littles series (John Peterson)

      Rosa Parks (Eloise Greenfield)

      Helen Keller (Margaret Davidson)

      The Case of the Elevator Duck (Polly Berends)

      Meet Martin Luther King, Jr. (James T. deKay)

      Tornado (Betsy Byars and Doron Ben Ami)

2   *Balto and the Great Race* (Elizabeth Kimmel)
    The Courage of Sarah Noble (Alice Dagliesh)
    Shark Lady (Ann McGovern and Ruth Chew)
    The Box Car Children series (Gertrude Warner)
    Stone Fox (John Reynolds Gardiner)

3   *Sarah Plain and Tall series* (Patricia MacLachlan)
    The Shoeshine Girl (Clyde Robert Bulla)
    Ramona Quimby, Age 8 (Beverly Cleary)
    Chocolate Touch (Patrick Skene)

PROFICIENCY TESTS

To ensure your students' success in this program, it is essential that you maintain the proper pace of instruction. From time to time, you will need to stop teaching so that you can evaluate how your students are doing. Your evaluations will take two forms: informal observations of your students' classroom performance and formal assessment through a series of curriculum-based proficiency tests. The evaluation process will guide your instructional planning by highlighting when to reteach key concepts or skills, when a student should be moved to a different reading group, or if the group is ready to continue in the sequence.

The handbook contains a total of thirteen proficiency tests, each with a spelling and reading section, and each administered over several days. The spelling section contains lists of phonograms, phonetic words, red words, and sentences for dictation. The reading section consists of phonograms, phonetic words, red words, and passages of text for students to read aloud. The instructional sequence will let you know when to stop and administer a test.

For each student, record a summary of your classroom observations and the proficiency test results on the Proficiency Test Summary Form that can be found on page 153 or downloaded from the PAF website. In scoring the proficiency tests, focus on the kinds and patterns of errors your students make. With the exception of red words, you do not need to jot down specific words that students misspell, only the area of confusion. For example, if a child writes or reads *pen* for *pin*, make note of the i/e confusion, not the words *pen* and *pin*.

Create an assessment folder for each student in which you keep completed tests and the Proficiency Test Summary Forms. These folders will serve as a record of your students' progress and as a useful resource to share with parents.

What follows here is more-detailed information about administering and scoring the two parts of the test.

Spelling (Administer to Students as a Group)

The spelling subtest is an opportunity to assess your students' spelling, as well as their handwriting, punctuation, and capitalization. Before the test, take down or cover your red word chart. Administer the test by giving the dictation as you do in your daily lessons, but do not provide any help.

When you review the spelling subtest, look for the following types of spelling errors:
- Confusing individual sounds (*mat* for *mad, sput* for *spot*)
- Omitting letters or syllables (*luch* for *lunch, diffrent* for *different*)
- Not applying rules (*banck* for *bank*)
- Making incorrect spelling choices (*teecher* for *teacher*)

You should also note whether the handwriting is legible; specific letters that are poorly formed or reversed; and problems with line placement and spacing, both between and within words. Finally, look for errors in the use of lowercase and uppercase letters and punctuation marks.

Reading (Administer to Students Individually)

The reading subtest is an opportunity to evaluate your students' decoding skills and word recognition, as well as their reading fluency and comprehension. There are two parts to the reading subtest: reading isolated words and reading passages of text from the Merrill Skills Books. Before you administer the test, make two copies each of the single-word reading list and the text selection. You will use one copy to take notes and record errors while each student reads. Have a pencil available in case the student wants to divide words.

Single Word Reading

On this portion of the test, the students read a page of isolated words divided into three sections: phonetic, multisyllable, and red words. The first six proficiency tests also contain a section of isolated phonograms. When students have difficulty reading multisyllable words, encourage them to divide the words and note whether they apply the rules of syllable division that you have taught. Analyze the misread words to determine what kinds of errors were made. Can the student read one-syllable words but not multisyllable words? Does the student omit sounds (*help* for *helps, let* for *left*), substitute sounds (*big* for *beg*), or insert sounds (*hand* for *had*)? Put one check above the words that the student recognizes automatically and two checks above the words that are sounded out.

Text Reading

On the next portion of the test, the students read specific passages and answer questions from the Merrill Skills Books. For the first five administrations of the reading subtest, have your students read and answer the comprehension questions orally. After the fifth test, have them read the questions to themselves and circle their answers.

Make note of the quality of the reading. Is the student reading accurately, but slowly? Is the student reading too quickly? Is the student reading word by word, or with proper phrasing and intonation? The following notations can be used to help you record specific errors.

- Substitutions: Write the student's substitution above the text.
- Omissions: Circle the omitted text or put a slash through omitted punctuation marks.
- Insertions: Use a caret (^) and write the inserted text.
- Self-Corrections: Write *SC*.
- Ignoring Punctuation: Put a slash through any punctuation marks that are ignored.
- Repetitions: Put a wavy line under the repeated text. If it is repeated more than once, add additional lines.

When filling out the Proficiency Test Summary Form, remember to record your observations of each student's reading comprehension of the text in the daily lessons, as well as each student's performance on the proficiency test.

Analysis of Data

The proficiency tests are curriculum-based and should be used to guide the pace of your instruction. Do not proceed to the next level in the instructional sequence until the majority of your students have mastered 90 percent of the material on a test. If one-third or more of your students find any concepts too difficult, reteach them to the class as a whole. You may also need to provide one-to-one assistance to some students to address their individual needs.

Here are some effective activities to provide extra review and practice:

- Repeat prior spelling dictations
- Provide additional supervised handwriting practice
- Have students reread word lists from Stepping Up in Reading (to improve decoding and word recognition skills)
- Have students reread stories from earlier levels in the Merrill Readers (to improve fluency)

If this level of proficiency has not been reached, consider the following questions:

- Have I allocated enough time for the implementation of the program?
- Has my pace of instruction been too fast?
- Have I provided sufficient opportunities for practice and reinforcement?
- Have I grouped my students appropriately or were the instructional levels of the students too diverse for one group?

If students are having comprehension problems, ask yourself these questions:

- Are they applying the reading strategies I have been modeling?
- Are they reading accurately and with sufficient fluency?
- Are there oral language issues?
- Do they have memory or attention problems?

When students cannot understand the vocabulary or grammar of what they read, there may be an underlying oral language problem. Consider referring such students to a language specialist for evaluation. The ability to understand spoken language will affect reading comprehension. For students with memory or attention problems, try to reduce the distractions in your classroom, and to provide them with seating close to you so that you can help them refocus during lessons. Students with memory and attention problems also benefit when you stop often to ask questions.

Finally, in addition to using the proficiency tests, many teachers find it useful to quantitatively measure students' progress in decoding and word recognition from year to year. For this purpose, you can download and use a different assessment tool, the PAF Test of Single Word Reading.

 After administering a Proficiency Test, remove cards from your review pack that contain material your students have mastered. The pack should change in content rather than continually grow in size.

PROFICIENCY TEST SUMMARY

Name _____ Date _____ Test # _____

Teacher _____ Grade _____

SPELLING

Red Words

Handwriting

Punctuation and Capitalization

_____

READING

Single Word Reading

Red Words

Text Reading

Instructional Goals

PROFICIENCY TEST SUMMARY

Name ___Dana Marks_____ **Date** __12/7_____ **Test** ___#3____

Teacher __Mrs. Dietch_____ **Grade** _1_____

SPELLING

Confusing o/u

Dropping last consonant when adding suffix s

Red Words

goes

Handwriting

Excellent letter formation but spacing between words poor

Punctuation and Capitalization

Used capitals for beginning of sentences but not names

Left off question mark

READING

Single Word Reading

Read one-syllable words at the word recognition level.

Slowed down to decode words with suffixes but was accurate.

Red Words

good

Text Reading

In class, Dana reads accurately but still word by word with little expression. At this level, however, this does not seem to be impacting her comprehension. Answered both questions on test correctly.

Instructional Goals

- Reinforce use of fingers to help with spacing when writing.
- Put small keyword cards for o and u on her desk for reference.
- During dictation, ask Dana for root word when dictating words with suffixes.
- Provide extra practice reading words lists with suffixes.

I.   **Spelling**

c   d   t   ă   l   s   h   f   m   p   r   b   v   j   n   y-

fat	sad	can	jam	pan	had
cap	tags	cats	bad	map	yams

I am mad at you.

Jan has your hat and bag.

Dad pats Rags.

The man ran to Sam's van.

Dan had a nap.

II.   **Oral Reading**

Single Word Reading (See following page.)

Text Reading: Merrill Skills Book – *I Can*, page 93

n c f d j t v a b

l r s p h m g y

---

sad	ham	fat	gas	and
at	ran	dad	sat	cats
man	jam	van	fan	tags
bad	had	yam	lap	pats
can	am	nap	hat	naps

---

the	you	I	your	to

I.   **Spelling**

w -x ĭ z ŭ qu b j ă y- p f h d n l v t r g s m

big	him	but	wax	hit	zip
if	quiz	live	quit	wins	runs

Fix Jim's cup.

Are they in the bus?

Give us six of his bags.

I said to put it up.

Did your kids have fun?

II.   **Oral Reading**

Single Word Reading (See following page.)

Text Reading: Merrill Skills Book – *Dig In*, page 93

d   l   t   s   g   m   a   r

v   n   h   c   z   u   x   i

w   k   qu   b   j   y   p   f

---

big   sun   us   mix   lives

if   dug   him   hit   wags

up   did   run   give   hugs

his   but   zip   have   wins

bus   six   fun   quit   kids

---

put   they   said   of   are

I.   **Spelling**

ch   ĭ   j   -x   ŭ   th   b   qu   ă   ĕ   v   d   ŏ   z   y-   w

Write the letter that says / ī / at the end of a one-syllable word. (y)
Write the *doing* suffix. (-ing)

me	got	so	my	top	men
hot	into	then	much	gets	fixing

Mr. Chin goes to bed at ten.

Tom can go to the ranch by bus.

Dr. Fox was very red from the sun.

Is he doing his math?

We were going to have lunch with them.

Have the children write the lowercase alphabet in order. Give the test in a room where the alphabet has been covered and no model of the alphabet is visible.

II.   **Oral Reading**

Single Word Reading (See following page.)

Text Reading: Merrill Skills Book – *Catch On,* page 111

e o j x i b qu f

h m v u r t g l

p z n y a s w d

---

red	men	such	kicked
us	lot	with	packed
my	let	them	telling
get	by	this	mixing
bed	bath	sick	locked
but	back	much	missed
got	well	catch	pitching

---

from was said of they were

I.   Spelling

ĕ   sh   ch   ŭ   ĭ   -ung   ŏ   -ang   qu   th   -ong   y-   ă   -x

Write the *doing* suffix. (-ing)
Write the suffix that says /iz/ as in *dresses*. (-es)

end	ship	hung	land	rang	went
shy	thing	sandbox	singing	rushes	bangs

I can't hang up the shelf by myself.
Who is doing the lunch dishes?
Don't send the cash to Ms. King yet.
Mrs. Long was fishing by the school.
She won't give me the ring.

Give each student a copy of the following words and have each write the contractions.

do not	are not	have not	will not
cannot	is not	did not	was not

II.   Oral Reading

Single Word Reading (See following page.)

Text Reading: Merrill Skills Book – *Get Set,* page 103

> Question #17: Ask the child to draw a circle around the sentence that tells what the whole story is about.

> Question #18: Ask the child to draw a circle around the words that complete the sentence and tell what happened in the story.

| e | u | a | x | i | qu | o |

| sh | ch | th | ong | ang | ing | ung |

---

long	hung	sings	picnic
end	shelf	wishes	rabbit
she	bang	fishing	until
land	shop	inches	lesson
song	wind	ringing	magnet
went	thing	myself	sudden

| who | don't | wasn't | won't |
| school | Mrs. | Mr. | Ms. |

I.   **Spelling**

ŭ   sh   qu   ŏ   -ank   ch   ĕ   -ink   ĭ   -unk   ă

Write the suffix that means *more.* (-er)

Write the *past time* suffix. (-ed)

Write the *doer* suffix. (-er)

Write the two suffixes that mean *more than one.* (-s, -es)

milk	help	best	ask	left	must
next	thank	gifts	faster	lasted	melted

Don't go into the school by yourself.

I think they fixed the fish tank.

Mrs. Sands wants to go to the bank.

Who just bumped into me?

Ben said he wanted a desk.

II.   **Oral Reading**

Single Word Reading (See following page.)

Text Reading: Merrill Skills Book – *Get Set,* page 120

Question #19: Ask the child to draw a circle around the sentence that tells what the whole story is about.

Question #20: Ask the child to draw a circle around the words that complete the sentence and tell what happened in the story.

a   e   ch   u   i   th   o

sh   ink   ang   unk   ank   ong   ung

---

must	desk	longer	summer
help	felt	landed	better
camp	think	jumped	contest
just	herself	banker	after
left	pitcher	melted	dinner
west	thanked	quicker	dentist
next	singer	missed	under
junk	asked	faster	winter

| want | were | who | was |

I.   **Spelling**

ă ar ŏ ĭ or qu ank ĕ ong unk all ŭ ang

Write the suffix that means *more*. (-er)
Write the suffix that means *the most*. (-est)

flag	north	March	forgive	after	smartest
begin	open	music	finish	seven	plastic

My sister is smaller than I am.

Mrs. Winter's car never starts in the morning.

They were glad someone got that hard job done.

There are spots that won't come off my shorts.

None of us belong to the club.

What is the longest river?

II.   **Oral Reading**

Single Word Reading (See following page.)

Text Reading: Merrill Skills Book – *Step Up,* page 101

> Have the child read the story aloud, read the questions
> silently, and circle the answers.

ar	qu	e	all	o	i
th	a	or	ch	u	sh
sm	sn	sl	st	sp	spl

---

dark	short	flying	calling
glad	clock	planted	hardest
flag	blank	tallest	glasses
sled	sport	parked	forget
still	snack	spelling	corner
north	smart	started	garden
stamp	March	smaller	morning

---

of	none	what	come	done
want	there	some	one	off

I.   **Spelling**

Write the suffix that means *the most.* (-est)

Write the suffix that means *without.* (-less)

Write the suffix that means *more.* (-er)

Write the suffix that means *full of.* (-ful)

tell	sky	grass	fell	stuff	twelve
swims	harmful	spotless	crushed	printer	pretend

April comes after March.

The glasses are filled with fresh milk.

Where were you walking to this morning?

Bring some drinks for the camping trip.

Are you still not talking to your friend?

I am well and thankful for your help.

II.   **Oral Reading**

Single Word Reading (See following page.)

Text Reading: Merrill Skills Book – *Step Up,* page 115

> Have the child read the story aloud, read the questions
> silently, and circle the answers.

swim	spring	strongest	over
frog	trying	smelled	even
trip	called	scratches	never
dress	crosses	freshest	music
horse	bringing	printed	seven
grass	yelled	finish	problem
drink	helpful	paper	belong
twins	twisted	begin	traffic
twelve	harmless	river	spider

---

opened	visiting	invented	polished
thundering	happened	gardener	pretending

---

where   talking   were   friend   full   walk

I.   **Spelling**

life   these   chose   cute   came   mile

rode   quite   hoping   bravest   careful   used

Write the question words. (who, what, when, where, why)

Why couldn't their mom be here on time?

Where are those five cubes to use with this game?

Are you sure they are coming over later?

There are no planes taking off because of the storm.

When would you like to go and vote?

My friend's home is closer to school than mine.

II.   **Oral Reading**

Single Word Reading (See following page.)

Text Reading: Merrill Skills Book – *Lift Off,* page 117

> Have the child read the story aloud, read the questions
> silently, and circle the answers.

smoke	whale	quite	became
here	cute	hoped	inside
made	gave	bravest	whisper
ride	state	tired	mistake
joke	while	using	entire
use	these	hopeful	arcade
like	white	taking	polite
same	which	driver	costume
fire	those	careless	escape

---

computer	inviting	behaved	confusing

---

could	sure	where	what	couldn't
should	their	would	who	because

I.   **Spelling**

stay	ugly	keep	tiny	mail	luck
airplane	painter	boating	brightest	rained	slowly

Does this pretty tree only grow along the east coast?

Should we meet across from the snack bar?

Have you been sailing over there this year?

Don't leave until you put away your games.

Coach says he really needs each player to show up next week.

Maybe I can sleep over again Friday night.

II.   **Oral Reading**

Single Word Reading (See following page.)

Text Reading: Merrill Skills Book – *Lift Off,* page 131

> Have the child read the story aloud, read the questions
> silently, and circle the answers.

might	own	lightning	highway
fair	party	seemed	meanwhile
feet	alive	waited	below
flight	panda	amazing	reason
growth	body	quickly	shadow
dream	afraid	airport	seasons
street	baby	midnight	freedom
throw	ago	raincoat	tenderly
meat	alone	maybe	delightful
pair	feelings	weekend	frequently

---

following	delayed	eagerly	container
meaningful	carelessly	windowless	hopefully

---

been   again   pretty   does   only   against

I.   Spelling

huge	summer	chance	simple	strange	center
middle	package	planet	dinner	biggest	peaceful

The women laughed when the baby made a funny face.

Werc you able to call the builders that built their deck?

My ankle felt better once I stopped running.

The garbage gets picked up twice a week in the city.

That nice woman might be getting us more tickets.

People were lining up even before the store opened.

II.   Oral Reading

Single Word Reading

Text Reading: Merrill Skills Book – *Take Flight*, page 146

> Have the child read the story aloud, read the questions
> silently, and circle the answers.

space	jungle	explain
score	fable	monster
price	empty	address
edge	angle	hungry
peace	angry	excited
since	gentle	happened
title	children	explorer
before	decide	suddenly
rocket	practice	frightening
message	hundred	successful
except	village	brightened

---

women	once	building	only
built	laugh	woman	people

I.   **Spelling**

wrong	kind	world	knife	weight	almost
every	dirty	warmest	turned	powerful	different

The child told us she wrote an important letter to the president.

Many people find it interesting to study wild animals.

Both the girls were at the surprise birthday party on Saturday.

Can I count on you to also water the flowers around the house?

Eight of our friends always get together on Thursdays.

Do you know how many cups are in a quart?

II.   **Oral Reading**

Single Word Reading

Text Reading: Merrill Skills Book – *Take Flight*, page 159

> Have the child read the story aloud, read the questions
> silently, and circle the answers.

south	thousand	without
write	perhaps	ourselves
worst	allow	however
wrote	perfect	continent
crowd	written	difficult
weight	quarters	holiday
knight	knocked	remember
bird	kinder	yesterday
behind	hurtful	energy
disturb	coldest	electric
person	warning	emergency

---

many	water	any
together	anyone	altogether

I.   Spelling

join	dawn	soon	carry	nothing	other
bears	trying	learned	cities	wonderful	understood

My son enjoyed learning how to count coins.

I heard that there is a great drawing class on Monday afternoons.

Do you believe that my brother ate half the pie already?

I am sorry that you have to get up really early tomorrow.

Many families hurried from their homes after the earthquake.

Buy some warm sweaters and gloves for the cold weather.

II.   Oral Reading

Single Word Reading

Text Reading: Merrill Skills Book – *Break Through,* page 146

> Have the child read the story aloud, read the questions
> silently, and circle the answers.

head	narrow	laziest
earth	August	annoying
field	heavy	enjoyable
wear	healthy	carrying
choice	author	earlier
lawn	foolish	happiness
break	moisten	government
meant	woodwind	discovery
fault	breakfast	dinosaur
spoil	greatest	astronaut
cause	thawed	neighborhood

| father | buy | half |
| grandfather | buyer | halfway |

I.   **Spelling**

grew	hours	drew	thumb	often	nature
honest	picture	future	castle	threw	avenue

Are you certain that the newspapers are tied up?

The water was too rough to take a boat ride around the island.

Is it true that only a few students could solve the new puzzle?

The Atlantic and Pacific Oceans border the United States.

Does listening to ghost stories scare you?

Are you tough enough to go on a mountain climbing adventure?

Have the students write the months of the year in sequence.

II.   **Oral Reading**

Single Word Reading

Text Reading: Have the child read to you the next section of the book you are using in class. Read at least one full page but less than a whole chapter of the book you are using in class. Be sure the child stops at a logical place in the narrative. Ask one or two questions to check comprehension.

comb	daughter	exhibit
juice	whistle	continue
knew	mountain	protection
group	guilty	jewelry
fruit	thoughtful	paragraph
caught	rescued	conclusion
brought	softened	transportation
honor	honesty	alphabetize
fasten	overdue	manufacture
plumber	decision	population
castle	permission	temperature
certain	signature	imagination

| island | ocean | enough |
| rough | toughest | Wednesday |

APPENDIX

Handwriting

Handwriting is an essential part of a multisensory curriculum. Early in the program, you will need to teach your students how to write each letter as they learn its sound. Until they can form all letters accurately and automatically, you should provide ongoing instruction and opportunities for supervised practice. The following pages contain specific instructions for teaching print and cursive.

There are six basic principles of handwriting instruction.

1. **Each letter is introduced with the motor pattern and the sound** in order to develop a strong automatic connection between three modalities: visual (letter form), auditory (letter sounds), and kinesthetic (how to write the letter). The simultaneous teaching of motor patterns and sounds is a key component of multisensory instruction.

2. **Handwriting is taught and practiced under the direct supervision of the teacher,** who provides immediate feedback and models correct letter formation. Handwriting is never assigned as independent work or homework.

3. **The instructional sequence for teaching handwriting is trace, copy, and write from memory.** Children trace the letter, copy the letter, and, to complete the lesson, write the letter from memory, all under the direction of the teacher.

4. **Motor patterns are always introduced through the large muscles of the arm and shoulder** rather than through the small muscles of the hand. Using large muscles helps children feel the changes in direction necessary to form each letter. Also, using large muscles helps children remember letter formations, because large muscle memory is extremely powerful. You never forget how to ride a bike or swim.

5. **Letters are grouped according to motor patterns.** For example, one group of letters is referred to as two o'clock letters, because each letter in the group is formed by starting at the 2 on an imaginary clock. The two o'clock letters are c, a, d, g, q, s, and f.

6. **Language is used to teach and reinforce handwriting** by having the teacher verbalize instructions for forming each letter. Children are told how to move their hands to produce the letter forms. Many children cannot learn the motor patterns for writing by simply copying letters and must receive verbal instructions.

In order to give verbal instructions on how to form the letters, you will need to establish certain reference points with your class. First, be sure all the desks in the classroom are facing forward. Next, using cloth tape, place a green line on the side of the board and on every desk. In classrooms with group tables rather than individual desks, give each student a 12-by-18-inch oaktag mat and place a green line on the left side. When giving verbal instructions, you will be able to tell your students to move their hands toward or away from the green, rather than to the left or right.

Also, to help you give verbal instructions, you will need a way to refer to each of the writing lines. In the handwriting books, the four writing lines have been given names: hat line, belt line, writing line, and shoe line. By teaching these names to your students and referring to them in your verbal instructions, you will help the children form letters with proper size and placement. For example, you may instruct the students to place their pencils on the belt line and pull down to the writing line. Be sure that your classroom board is marked with the same four writing lines and with a green line to the left.

Although the exact wording of the verbal instructions may vary from teacher to teacher, it is important that your own instructions remain consistent. As your students begin to form letters accurately and automatically, you can give less detailed instructions. Eventually stop giving instructions altogether.

Because this is a multisensory program, you will need to teach each motor pattern along with the sound of the letter, following the instructions on pages 9 and 10. When teaching print, you will use three different kinds of writing paper, each one requiring your students to produce smaller letters. On the first kind of paper, the lines are ruled ½" apart and the paper is aligned horizontally so that young students can place an entire sentence on one line.

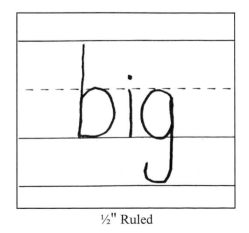

½" Ruled

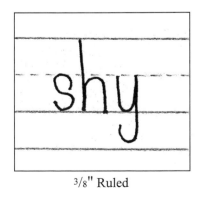

3/8" Ruled

Once your students have learned the twenty-six lower-case letters, you should begin using paper with lines ruled ⅜" apart, still aligned horizontally. Finally, when your students have learned all the lower-case and capital letters, at the end of first grade or beginning of second grade) you will begin using paper with lines ruled ³⁄₁₆" apart and oriented vertically.

3/16" Ruled

Whenever you introduce a new kind of writing paper, be sure to provide a model of the alphabet on that paper for the children to trace and copy. After this step, they can begin to use the paper independently.

Teach your students to hold their pencils about one inch from the point and at a forty-five-degree angle to the table. The proper three-finger grip is to hold the pencil between the thumb and the index finger and support it with the middle finger. When children are first learning to write, you may put molded finger grips on their pencils to help them learn the correct finger positions. Also, teach your students that writing requires both hands: one to hold the pencil and the other to hold the paper.

Once your students can write all the lower-case and capital letters clearly and automatically, you no longer need to teach handwriting on a daily basis. Instead, provide handwriting lessons as needed, when you see weaknesses in your students' written work. Be sure that your class understands that you expect good handwriting in all writing assignments, and be consistent in holding your students to this expectation.

While you are teaching your students to write printed letters, you may choose to teach them to write numerals as well. The Handwriting Program for Numerals contains pages for tracing, copying, and writing numerals from memory, along with basic mathematical concepts.

Lower-Case Print Letter Groups

It is important to teach your students to print letters using one stroke, as this will facilitate learning to write in cursive. For example, a child who learns to form a **d** using one stroke and practices this motor pattern in the primary grades will have no problem learning to form a cursive *d* , as the motor patterns are nearly identical. The only printed letters that cannot be taught in one stroke are **t, f, x,** and **k** (use these letters in the new sentences below, please)**.**

Before you teach your class to form the letters, you should explain that each of the lines on the paper has a name. Use the first page in the Handwriting Program for Print to teach the names of the four lines. By using the names of the lines and the green line as reference points, you will be able to describe your hand movements as you demonstrate how to write each letter. For example, while teaching the letter *v*, you might say: *Put your pencil on the belt line, slant away from the green, and then slant up.* Try to use language that guides the children in forming their letters.

 If you would like examples of verbalizations for the print letters, you can download them from the PAF website.

Two O'Clock Letters

The two o'clock letters are the only printed letters that do not begin on a line. Have your students imagine where the 2 would be on a clock drawn between the belt and shoe lines. Tell your students that whenever you say *two o'clock,* they should put their pencils slightly below the belt line and go up and over to the green. The **f** is a *tall* two o'clock letter that begins under the hat line.

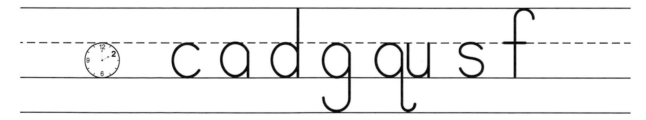

Tall Letters

Tell your students that when you say *tall letter,* they should put their pencils on the hat line and pull down to the writing line. The **t** is a *teenage* letter.

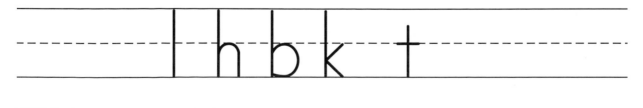

Short Letters

Tell your students that when they hear *short letter,* they should put their pencils on the belt line and pull straight down.

Slanty Letters

Tell your students that when they hear *slanty letter,* they should put their pencils at the belt line and slant down and away from the green.

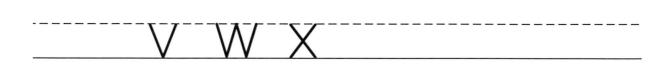

Letters That Are Not in a Group

The letter *o* is taught as a twelve o'clock letter in order to form it the way the letter is written in cursive. The letters *e* and *z* begin with a line that goes away from the green.

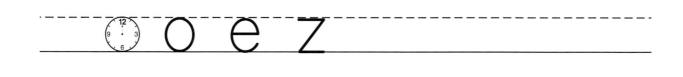

Capital Print Letter Groups

Most capital letters begin with a straight line down from the hat line. The number of strokes is indicated in parentheses over each letter.

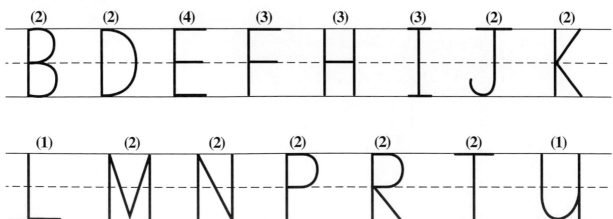

Capital Two O'Clock Letters

Tell the children to put their pencils slightly under the hat line when they hear *two o'clock* for a capital letter.

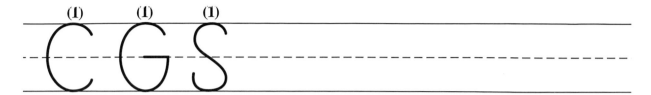

Capital Twelve O'Clock Letters

Tell the children to put their pencils on the hat line when they hear *twelve o'clock* for a capital letter.

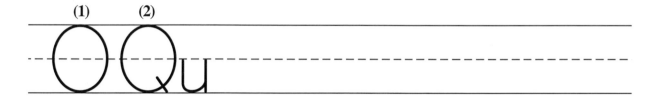

Capital Slanty Letters

Tell the children to put their pencils on the hat line and slant away from the green when they hear *slanty letter* for a capital.

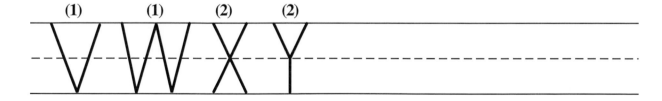

Letters Not Taught in a Group

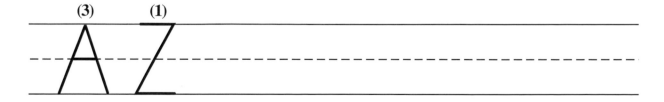

Teaching Cursive

You should start teaching cursive in the beginning of third grade, regardless of where your children are in the Instructional Sequence. Since the children will already know the sounds of the letters, cursive instruction is not part of the daily multisensory lesson. You should set aside time for separate cursive lessons. While your students are learning cursive, they will continue to work through the Instructional Sequence, completing their written work in print.

Many of the basic principles used in teaching print apply to teaching cursive as well: students should work under the supervision of a teacher; group letters by motor pattern; introduce the letters by having students use large muscles; give verbal instructions and have the children trace, copy, and then write the letters from memory. One difference in teaching cursive is that the children will say the letter name rather than its sound while learning the motor patterns.

As when teaching print, arrange all the desks in you classroom facing forward, and be sure your students use proper posture and pencil grip. Have them orient their papers at a forty-five-degree angle from the edge of their desks and parallel to their writing arms. Most right-handed children produce letters slanting toward the right-hand corner of the page; most left-handed children produce letters slanting toward the left-hand corner. The direction of the slant of the letters is less important than its consistency: always to the right corner or always to the left. To accommodate the needs of both your left- and right-handed students, the Handwriting Program for Cursive books come in two versions. The books are identical except for the slant of the letters.

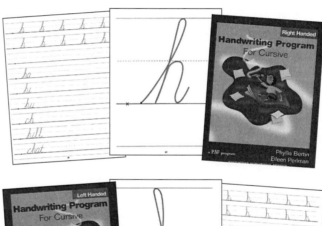
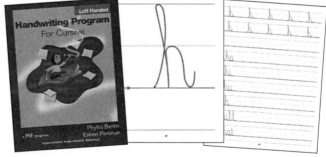

The handwriting books begin by teaching the twenty-six lower-case letters. While your students are learning these letters, they should use ⅜" ruled paper for extra practice. Once the students know all the lower-case letters, they should begin doing spelling dictations (and gradually all their written work in cursive, using ³⁄₁₆" ruled paper). You may have to shorten dictations until your students can produce cursive, letters quickly and accurately. Your students can print the capital letters until they have learned the motor patterns.

While the children are making the transition from print, you can give them homework in which they copy printed text into cursive. They can practice copying their red words, and you can supply a short paragraph for them to copy. Be sure to give them the ³⁄₁₆" paper for this practice.

Lower-Case Cursive Letter Groups

All lower-case letters start on the writing line, and all but four bridge letters (*b, v, w,* and *o*) end on the writing line. Because bridge letters do not end on the writing line, they are difficult to connect to the next letter and require special emphasis. Connecting bridge letters to rocket letters, such as *i* or *h*, is particularly difficult. Teach children to come down so the bridge sags (*b*), rather than going straight across the belt line (*b*). In this way they will approach the next letter from the usual direction, from the bottom up. Both large and small models of specific bridge connections are provided in the handwriting books.

 If you would like examples of verbalizations for the cursive letters, you can download them from the PAF website.

Two O'Clock Letters

Teach children that when they hear *two o'clock,* they should swing up and over to two o'clock, stop, and go back toward the green line.

Tall Letters

Teach the children to make a curved line up to the hat line and pull straight down when they hear *tall letter*.

Rocket Letters

Teach children to swing to the belt line and to come down on the same line when they hear *rocket letter*.

Hill Letters

Teach children to swing up to the belt line and make a hill when they hear *hill letter*.

$$\mathcal{N} \; \mathcal{M} \; \mathcal{N} \; \mathcal{Y} \; \mathcal{X} \; \mathcal{Z}$$

Twelve O'Clock Letter

$$\mathcal{O}$$

Capital Cursive Letter Groups

All capitals are connected to the next letter except $\mathcal{D}, \mathcal{O}, \mathcal{P}, \mathcal{V}, \mathcal{W},$ and $\mathcal{X}.$

Several capitals end like a boat bottom. Demonstrate this association to facilitate the verbalization *make a boat*.

All capitals begin at the top except these:

$$\mathcal{S} \; \mathcal{D} \; \mathcal{L} \; \mathcal{J}$$

These three letters have the same motor patterns as their lower-case partners.

$$\mathcal{A} \; \mathcal{C} \; \mathcal{O}$$

The following letters are grouped for similar motor patterns.

$\mathcal{I}$ $\mathcal{F}$ $\mathcal{P}$ $\mathcal{R}$ $\mathcal{B}$

$\mathcal{H}$ $\mathcal{K}$ $\mathcal{M}$ $\mathcal{N}$

$\mathcal{U}$ $\mathcal{V}$ $\mathcal{W}$ $\mathcal{Y}$ $\mathcal{Q}u$ $\mathcal{Z}$

Each of the remaining letters has its own motor pattern.

$\mathcal{D}$ $\mathcal{E}$ $\mathcal{L}$ $\mathcal{X}$

Left-Handed Children

Left-handed children make certain instinctive movements when learning to write, different from those made by right-handed children. For example, most left-handed children, or lefties, draw horizontal lines from right to left rather than left to right. This is because all children draw horizontal lines by starting on their nondominant side and moving toward their writing hand. Likewise, most lefties draw circles clockwise rather than counterclockwise. This is because all children draw circles by beginning with an upward stroke that moves toward the body midline. For lefties, these movements feel as normal and comfortable as the more familiar writing movements feel to righties.

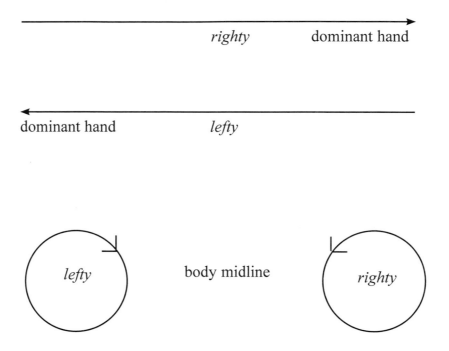

Left-handed children also have a natural tendency to scan pages from right to left, rather than left to right. They must overcome this inclination in order to read and write successfully. Beginning in preschool, lefties should be trained to work automatically from left to right. Mark the left side of the blackboard and the students' desks with a green line as a reference point for where to begin work. Be sure to include specific instructions to draw horizontal lines from left to right (away from the green) and to draw circles in a counterclockwise direction (toward the green). Teaching children to make circles with a counterclockwise movement will reduce the frequency of reversing the two o'clock letters.

One of the most natural movements in the cursive writing of left-handed children is a back slant. Most children produce cursive letters at a slant by placing their writing paper parallel to their writing arm. For righties the result is a forward slant, or letters leaning to the upper-right corner of the page. For lefties the result is a back slant, or letters leaning to the upper left.

Although the left-handed back slant is less common than the forward slant, it is equally acceptable and does not need to be changed. Instead, teach lefties to use their natural back slant by displaying a left-handed cursive alphabet in your classroom and by giving them appropriate letter models to trace from the Handwriting Program for Cursive. Some children—both lefties and righties—prefer to hold their writing paper perpendicular to the desk and write with no slant to their letters. You should allow your students to select whatever paper position and slant is most comfortable, as long as they are then consistent. Under no circumstances, however, should you encourage lefties to write with a forward slant, as this can result in undue strain and hooking of the wrist, a source of muscle tension and fatigue. Finally, be aware that smudging is often an unavoidable consequence of writing with the left hand.

Left-handed Alphabet

a b c d e f g h i j k l m

n o p q u r s t u v w x y z

A B C D E F H I J K L M

N O P Q u R S T U V W X Y Z

Lesson Plans

This section contains four blank lesson plan forms for your use, which can be downloaded, and three sample lessons. You will select one of the first three blank lesson plan forms, depending on which level you are teaching. They vary slightly in content: for example, the lesson plan for Levels 1 to 55 includes words to spell with the pocket chart, while the other two lesson plans do not. The fourth blank lesson plan form is to use when teaching any red word.

Each lesson plan form has five sections that correspond to the sequence of the daily lesson.
- **Review**: This section is simply a reminder to do the review using the card packs.
- **Introduction of New Material**: Jot down any materials you might need.
- **Spelling Dictation**: Write the words and sentences you have selected for dictation. You do not have to use all the spaces provided on the form. You can also use the lesson plan to keep track of errors.
- **Reading**: This is a place to record the pages you want to read with the children. You will write your questions and prompts for discussion directly in the Merrill Reader, not on this form.
- **Reinforcement**: Write down any activities and attach work sheets you plan to use.

After the four blank lesson plan forms you will find three sample lessons that demonstrate how to fill out these blank forms and how to create the comprehension lesson in the Merrill Reader.

Sample Lesson Plan I - Level 34 (Merrill Reader B)
This lesson introduces the short vowel *i*. At this early stage in the sequence, when the children are learning how to form the letters, the dictations are shorter than they will be later. That is why only one sentence has been chosen for dictation. The lesson for the story "Nat and the Map" has been planned around the main idea of a problem (Nat destroys Sam's map). Since the author offers no solution, the story lends itself to asking the children for a logical next step for Sam.

Sample Lesson Plan II - Level 73 (Merrill Book C)
This lesson introduces the letter *y* making the sound /ī/ at the end of a one-syllable word. Because there are only two pattern words, two sentences have been included for dictation. "Grandma's Story" is a version of "Henny Penny" (or "Chicken Little") and an excellent opportunity to present this classic fable. First, the children read the Merrill version and retell the narrative in sequence. Then read an illustrated version of "Henny Penny" to them. The lesson concludes with a discussion of which version of the story the children like better and why.

Sample Lesson Plan III - Level 171 (Merrill Book G)

This lesson is about learning to use twin consonants in the middle of two-syllable root words. "Different Kinds of Apes" is a nonfiction selection that offers the opportunity to model comprehension strategies, such as taking notes. As the children are reading the selection aloud, stop after each type of ape is described to ask the children what they have learned. Then, model converting the facts to notes on the board. The children can use the notes to verbally summarize what they have learned. The reinforcement activity requires them to go back to the text for specific information.

PAF LESSON PLAN
Levels 1-55

Date_____Level_____Skill_____

Review Packs for Reading and Spelling

_____

Introduction of New Material

PAF Handwriting Program for Print, pages_____

_____

Spelling Dictation

Words for pocket chart (2-3)*   _____   _____   _____

Words for paper (4-6)**   _____   _____   _____

                                        _____   _____   _____

Sentences (1-2)

1._____

2._____

_____

Reading:

First Steps In Reading   pages _____

Stepping Up In Reading   pages _____

Merrill Reader   pages _____

Merrill Skills Book   pages _____

_____

Reinforcement Activities

* Discontinue use of the pocket chart after you have taught all the letters of the alphabet (Level 55).
**In kindergarten, you may dictate fewer words and no sentences, depending on the children's needs.

PAF LESSON PLAN
Levels 56-158

Date_____Level_____Skill_____

Review Packs for Reading and Spelling

_____

Introduction of New Material

_____

Spelling Dictation

Words (6-9)   _____   _____   _____

                     _____   _____   _____

                     _____   _____   _____

Sentences (1-2)

1. _____

   _____

2. _____

   _____

_____

Reading

Stepping Up In Reading   pages _____

Merrill Reader   pages _____

Merrill Skills Book   pages _____

_____

Reinforcement Activities

PAF LESSON PLAN
Levels 159-215

Date_____Level_____Skill_____

Review Packs for Reading and Spelling

_____

Introduction of New Material

_____

Spelling Dictation

Words (6-9)   _____   _____   _____

_____   _____   _____

_____   _____   _____

Sentences (2-3)

1. _____

_____

2. _____

_____

3. _____

_____

_____

Reading

Stepping Up In Reading   pages _____

Merrill Reader Book   pages _____

Chapter Book   pages _____

Merrill Skills Book   pages _____

_____

Reinforcement Activities

PAF LESSON PLAN
Introduction of a Red Word

Date_____Level_____Skill _____

Review Packs for Reading and Spelling

_____

Introduction of New Material

_____

Spelling Dictation

Hide the red word card. Say the word and have children write the word on paper from memory, saying the word and letter names. Show the card. Repeat 3-4 times.

Sentences

1. _____

_____

2. _____

_____

3. _____

_____

_____

Reading

Stepping Up In Reading	pages _____
Merrill Reader Book	pages _____
Chapter Book	pages _____
Merrill Skills Book	pages _____

Reinforcement Activities

SAMPLE LESSON PLAN I
Level 34

Date ___11/2___   Level ___34___   Skill ___i (igloo)___

Review Packs for Reading and Spelling

Introduction of New Material

    PAF Handwriting Program for Print, pages ___36-7___

Ii
🏠
igloo

"This is an igloo. What is the first sound in igloo?" Check each child's pronunciation. "Now let's practice writing the sound /ĭ/."

Spelling Dictation

    Words for pocket chart (2-3)*   __it__   __him__   __did__

    Words for paper (4-6)**   __in__   __big__   __his__

                         __sits__   _____   _____

    Sentences (1-2)

1. __Sam sits in his van.__

2. _____

Reading

    First Steps In Reading   pages ___-___

    Stepping Up In Reading   pages ___19___

    Merrill Reader   pages ___5-8___

    Merrill Skills Book   pages ___2___

Reinforcement Activities

    Illustrate the story "Nat and the Map".

SAMPLE LESSON PLAN I
Level 34
Merrill Reader - Book B, *Dig In*

Before Reading: Today we're going to read another story about Nat. Do you remember how that cat always gets into mischief? Let's see what trouble Nat gets into today.

Nat and the Map

During Reading:

Sam had a map in the van.

Nat looks at it.

Nat hits and hits the map.

He hit it and bit it.

What just happened?

Sam had to look at the map.

It's in bits!

He looks at Nat.

Bad Nat!

It's bad to hit Sam's map!

How is Sam feeling? Why?
What might he do to solve his problem?

After Reading: Let's think of another title.
Sam's Problem / The Ripped Map

SAMPLE LESSON PLAN II
Level 73
Merrill Reader - Book C, *Catch On*

Date ___3/29___   Level ___73___   Skill ___-y (fly)___

Review Packs for Reading and Spelling

Introduction of New Material | -y / ø / fly | The sound /ī/ is spelled with a "y" at the end of a little word. The "y" is doing the job of the vowel.

Spelling Dictation

Words (6-9)   my   by   _____

Sentences (1-2)

1. That is not my laptop.

2. Can you be at the bus by ten?

Reading

Bring Henny Penny book.

Stepping Up In Reading   pages **80**
Merrill Reader   pages **85-88**
Merrill Skills Book   pages **-**

Reinforcement Activities

Stepping Up in Reading (pg 80)

Choose two phrases that answer the question "where" and use them in written sentences.

SAMPLE LESSON PLAN II
Level 73
Merrill Reader - Book C, *Catch On*

Before Reading: Discuss what children know about fables.
(moral/lesson characters = animals)
Today we're going to read a famous fable that has been
told many ways (versions)

Grandma's Story

Let's see how Grandma tells the story.

During
Reading :   Jan and Dan cooked lunch for
Grandma and Grandpa. Jan cut
ham an inch thick. Then she
mixed a punch. "I will fix hot
buns with a pinch of this and a
pinch of that," Dan said. "Then
Grandma will tell us a story."

This is Grandma's story.
Why did author put line here?

Little Red Hen was in the woods.
A nut fell and hit her. "The sky
fell on me!" she yelled. "I will go
tell the duck." So Little Red Hen
ran to tell the duck.

What is Little Red Hen's problem?

How do you think she is feeling?

86

"My, my, that's bad!" said the
duck. "Let's go tell the fat pig." So
the hen and the duck ran to tell
the pig. *What do you think will happen*
when they tell the pig?

"My, my," said the pig, "that's
bad! Let's go tell the horse." So
the hen, the duck, and the pig ran
to tell the horse.
What do you think will happen now?

"My, my, that's bad!" said the
horse to the hen. "Let's go tell the
fox."   *Is that a good idea? Why?*

The duck pecked at the latch on
the horse's pen. The hen, the duck,
and the pig got up on the horse's

87

Henny Penny
H. Werner Zimmermann

Read Aloud:

Now we're going to listen to how another author tells the same story → another version

Compare different endings.

What words could you use to describe the fox? (sly, clever) The other animals? (foolish) Why?

Discuss moral
Think for yourself
or
Don't believe everything you hear

Which version do you like better? Why?

Follow up: Read other "sly fox" tales aloud, such as "The Gingerbread Boy."

---

back. Then the bunch went into the woods to look for the fox.

"The sky fell on me!" said the hen to the fox.

The fox looked at the sky. Then she looked at the path. "No, it was not the sky that fell," said the fox. "Look, it's a little nut. A nut fell on you, Red Hen."

What did the fox do?
Was it a good idea to visit the fox? Why?

After Reading: Retell the story.
Read aloud: Henny Penny

88

SAMPLE LESSON PLAN III
Level 171
Merrill Reader - Book G, *Take Flight*

Date ___12 / 4_____ Level ___171_____ Skill Twin Consonants

Review Packs for Reading and Spelling

II. Introduction of New Material Put words with twin Consonants on board to read.
"We've been reading words with twin consonants. Today we will
spell some. You must remember the twin consonants."

Spelling Dictation

Words (6-9)

better	penny	gallon
rabbit	letter	address
sudden	bottom	

Sentences (2-3)

1. Some rabbits build nests.

2. Put your name and address on top
   of the letter.

3. _____

Reading

Stepping Up In Reading	pages 35
Merrill Reader	pages 69 - 75
Chapter Book	pages -
Merrill Skills Book	pages -

Reinforcement Activities

Complete the fact sheet after reading
"Different Sorts of Apes."

SAMPLE LESSON PLAN III

Level 171

Merrill Reader - Book G, *Take Flight*

Before Reading: (download photos of 4 apes)

Yesterday we read a story about a chimpanzee.
Today we will read some non-fiction about chimpanzees + 3 other types of apes.

Let's see what we learn about apes!

Different Sorts of Apes

During Reading:

Lots of people like monkeys and apes more than all the other zoo animals. Monkeys and apes may be kept in cages in the same part of the zoo. But they are not in the same family. One way to tell them apart is by the tail. Monkeys have tails. Apes do not.

There are a number of different sorts of apes. These are the gorilla, chimpanzee, orangutan, and gibbon.

Display pictures of apes + label them.

① Gorillas are the biggest of the apes. When they stand upright, they may be six feet tall. On the scales, they may go up to five hundred pounds.

What did we learn about the size of gorillas? (Paraphrase and write notes on board)

These big apes with long fangs and strange faces can never be tamed. In the jungle, they do not eat meat, but in the zoo they may begin to like it. They can stand upright on their back legs for a short time, but they travel on their hands and feet. At night, they make nests to sleep in.

What else have we learned about gorillas?

② Chimpanzees are smaller than gorillas and much smarter. They are not hard to train. One farmer

(Add to list)

74

---

is teaching a chimp to drive a jeep.

Tell me some facts about chimpanzees? (Add)

③ Orangutans are strange-looking apes with puffy cheeks and long red hair. They range from three to five feet tall.

What have we learned about how orangutans look? (Add)

④ Gibbons have longer arms than the other apes. In the jungle, they race from treetop to treetop, chattering as they go.

What have we learned about gibbons? (Add)

Apes do not always enjoy being kept in zoos. Pages of strange tales are printed about one gorilla named Bamboo who came to a zoo at the age of one. He had good care, but he was never tamed. He seemed to go into a rage whenever people looked at him. Then he would pound his chest with his fists. He would toss all sorts of things at people within range of his cage. Keepers didn't dare go into his cage when he was in such a rage.

What is main idea of paragraph? Find sentence with main idea (topic sentence). Discuss that Bamboo is an example → supports main idea

Gibbons, too, do not seem to enjoy zoo life. In fact, it is hard to keep them alive in zoos. Maybe they can't stop wishing for the free life they used to have in the treetops. What do you think?

Should animals be kept in zoos? Why?

After Reading: Use notes to discuss what has been learned about each ape.

Erase board and complete worksheet.

75

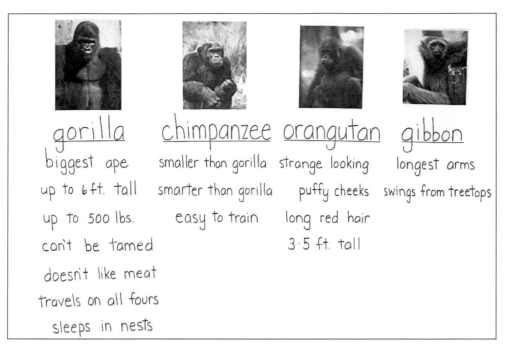

gorilla
biggest ape
up to 6 ft. tall
up to 500 lbs.
can't be tamed
doesn't like meat
travels on all fours
sleeps in nests

chimpanzee
smaller than gorilla
smarter than gorilla
easy to train

orangutan
strange looking
puffy cheeks
long red hair
3-5 ft. tall

gibbon
longest arms
swings from treetops

This is an example of the notes you might write on the board while your students are reading the text aloud and discussing it with you. You can explain that taking notes is a way to help the reader understand and remember information. Students can use the notes to summarize the information orally.

Book G
Level 171

Name _____

Go back to the book and find one fact about how each ape looks.
Write the facts in your own words in complete sentences.

orangutan _____
_____
_____

chimpanzee _____
_____
_____

gorilla _____
_____
_____

gibbon _____
_____
_____

This fact sheet is an example of a reinforcement activity your students can do independently. Encourage them to go back to the text to find the information and to write in complete sentences.

Instructional Sequence

**PREPARATION
FOR BOOK A** *(I Can)*
1. c (cat)
2. a (apple)
3. t (tiger)
4. d (dog)
5. g (girl)
6. s (sun)
7. f (fish)
8. m (moon)
9. l (lion)
10. Red Word: *a*
    Capital A
    Use of Capitals and Periods
11. h (hammer)
12. p (pumpkin)
13. n (nest)
14. Red Word: *I*
15. Plural s
16. Capital N
    Capitals for Names

BOOK A *(I Can)*
17. Red Word: *is*
18. Red Word: *the*
    Question Marks *for reading only*
19. Capital T
20. Capital D
21. j (jet)
    Exclamation Marks
    for reading only
22. b (boy)
23. r (robot)
24. Red Word: *to*
25. v (valentine)
26. s (tags)
    Capital J
27. Possessive s
28. y- (yarn)
29. Red Words: *you, your*
30. Capital Y
31. Capital S
32. Capital R
33. s (verb form)
    Capital F

PROFICIENCY TEST #1

BOOK B *(Dig In)*
34. i (igloo)
35. w (web)
36. Red Word: *said*
37. -x (box)
38. Question Marks
39. Red Word: *of*

40. Capital C
41. k (king)
42. z (zebra)
43. Capital P
44. u (umbrella)
45. Capital B
46. -ve (give)
    Capital G
47. qu (queen)
48. Red Word: *are*
49. Capital K
50. Red Word: *they*
51. Capital H
52. Capital M
    Red Word: *put*

PROFICIENCY TEST #2

BOOK C *(Catch On)*
53. o (octopus)
54. Red Word: *was*
    Capital W
55. e (elephant)
56. Suffix: -ing
57. Capital L
58. Red Word: *from*
    Capital O
59. Capital E
    -ll *for reading only*
60. Capital U
    -ff *for reading only*
61. -ss *for reading only*
    Red Word: *were*
62. Capital Z
    -ck *for reading only*
    Exclamation Marks
63. Capital Qu
    Final Double Consonants
    for reading only
64. Capital V
65. Red Word: *very*
    Suffix: -ed = /t/ *for reading only*
66. Compound Words
67. th (thin)
68. Red Word: *do*
69. Two-Letter Words
    (Long Vowel)
    Red Word: *goes*
70. ch (check)
71. Title: Mr.
72. -tch *for reading only*
73. -y (fly)
74. Title: Dr.

PROFICIENCY TEST #3

BOOK D *(Get Set)*
75. sh (ship)
76. Contractions
77. Red Words: *don't, won't*
78. -ang (gang), -ong (song)
    Red Word: *who*
79. -ing (ring)
    Title: Ms.
80. -ung (rungs)
    Red Word: *school*
81. Syllable Division: VCCV
82. Suffix: -es
83. -lf (elf), -nd (hand)
84. Title: Mrs.
85. -nt (tent)

PROFICIENCY TEST #4

86. Suffix: -er (*doer* suffix)
87. -ank (bank), -ink (pink),
    -unk (trunk)
88. -st (west)
89. Suffix: -er (*more*)
90. -sk (mask), -ft (gift)
91. -er (as in *after*)
92. Suffix: -ed = /ĭd/
93. Red Word: *want*
94. -lt (belt), -lk (milk)
95. -mp (stamp)
96. Suffix: -ed = /t/

PROFICIENCY TEST #5

BOOK E *(Step Up)*
97. Open & Closed Syllables
98. pl- (plant)
    Red Word: *what*
99. gl- (glass)
100. bl- (black)
101. Red Words: *one, done, none*
102. cl- (clock)
    Red Word: *there*
103. ar (star)
104. sl- (sleep)
    Red Words: *some, come*
105. Suffix: -est
106. fl- (flag)
107. sm- (smile), sn- (snail)
108. sp- (spot),
    spl- (splash) *for reading only*
109. or (corn)
110. R-Controlled Syllables
111. all (ball)
112. st- (stop)
    Red Word: *off*

PROFICIENCY TEST #6

113. Syllable Division: VCV
114. -ll
115. Suffix: -ed = /d/
116. sk- (skunk)
117. sw- (swing)
     Red Words: *walk, talk*
118. -ss
     Title: Miss
119. tw- (twelve)
     Red Word: *where*
120. tr- (truck)
     str- (straw) *for reading only*
121. cr- (crab),
     scr- (screw) *for reading only*
122. -ff
123. fr- (frog)
     Red Word: *friend*
124. dr- (drum)
125. gr- (green)
126. br- (brush)
127. pr- (pretzel),
     spr- (spring) *for reading only*
128. Red Word: *full*
129. Suffixes: -ful, -less

PROFICIENCY TEST #7

BOOK F *(Lift Off)*
130. a-e (snake)
131. Silent *e* Rule
132. Red Words: *could, would, should*
133. i-e (nine)
134. Nouns and Verbs
135. wh- (whale)
136. Red Word: *their*
     Homonyms: *their, there*
137. o-e (bone)
138. u-e (mule)
     Red Word: *sure*
139. e-e (these)
     Red Word: *because*
140. Silent *e* Syllables

PROFICIENCY TEST #8

---

141. ai (rain)
142. Spelling Choices a-e/ai
143. Homonyms: ai/a-e
144. -ay (gray)
     Red Word: *says*
145. ee (feet)
     Red Word: *been*
146. there *(in that place)*
147. ea (leaf)
148. Spelling Choices ee/ea
149. Homonyms: Long *e*
     Red Word: *does*

150. oa (boat)
     Homonyms: road, rode
151. ow (snow)
152. Vowel Team Syllables
153. -ck
154. -y *(as in candy)*
155. Adjectives
     Suffix: -y
     Red Word: *pretty*
156. Adverbs
     Suffix: -ly
     Red Word: *only*
157. a (as in *asleep*)
     Red Words: *again, against*
158. igh (light)

PROFICIENCY TEST #9

BOOK G *(Take Flight)*
159. -en (as in *kitchen*)
     for reading only
160. Red Words: *woman, women*
161. -et (as in *basket*)
162. Doubling Rule
163. -ore (store)
164. Soft *c* (as in *ice*)
165. -ce (as in *dance*)
     Red Word: *once*
166. Syllable Division:
     VCCCV
     Red Word: *laugh*
167. Special Syllable Endings
     -ble, -fle, -gle, -kle
168. Special Syllable Endings
     -dle, -ple, -tle, -zle
     Red Word: *people*
169. Soft *g* (as in *magic*)
     for reading only
170. -dge
     Red Words: *build, built*
171. Twin Consonants
     for spelling only
172. -age (as in *cabbage*)

PROFICIENCY TEST #10

---

173. -ild (as in *child*)
     -ind (as in *kind*)
174. -old (as in *cold*)
     -ost (as in *most*)
     -olt (as in *colt*)
175. er (fern)
     Red Words: *any, many*
176. wr- (wrist)
177. Multisyllable Root Words
178. eigh (eight)
179. ur (purple)

180. kn- (knee)
181. ir (bird)
182. ou (cloud)
183. ow (brown)
184. al- (as in *almost*)
     Red Word: *together*
185. w (or) (as in *work*)
186. w (ar) (as in *warm*)
     Red Word: *water*

PROFICIENCY TEST #11

BOOK H *(Break Through)*
187. -rr (as in *arrow*)
188. o (as in *love*)
     Red Word: *father*
189. ea (feather)
190. Y Rule
     Red Word: *buy*
191. ea (steak)
192. -ear (earth)
193. au (faucet) *for reading only*
194. aw (saw)
195. oo (moon)
196. Adding *s* to *y* words
197. oo (book)
     Red Word: *half*
198. ie (chief), ie (pie)
199. oi (poison)
200. oy (boy)

PROFICIENCY TEST #12

---

201. aught (as in *caught*)
     for reading only
     ought (as in *bought*)
     for reading only
202. Red Words:
     rough, tough, enough
203. ue (blue)
     Days of the Week
     Red Word: *Wednesday*
204. gu- (as in *guitar*)
205. -tion (as in *fraction*)
206. Silent Letters
207. ew (news)
208. ou (soup), ui (fruit)
     for reading only
209. Months of the Year
210. -sion (as in *vision*)
     for reading only
211. -sion (as in *mansion*)
     for reading only
212. -ain (as in *mountain*)
213. -ture (as in *picture*)
214. Red Words: *ocean, island*
215. ph (phone) *for reading only*

PROFICIENCY TEST #13

Rules of Thumb

English is a fascinating and rich language. Throughout its history, it has borrowed words and features from other languages, causing it to continuously expand and evolve. Because it has been influenced by so many languages, English can sometimes seem confusing and complex. Many people view English as a language with more exceptions than rules, one lacking a clear system for the spelling of its words.

In fact, there are many underlying patterns and rules to English, and most of its spellings are predictable. And it is easier for students to learn a handful of new rules than to memorize the spelling of countless words. Also, be assured that as your students grow familiar with the rules of thumb below, their skills will improve not only in spelling but in reading as well.

Rules for Letter Sounds

When the letter *c* comes before the letters *e, i,* or y, it always makes the sound /s/ (city).

When the letter *g* comes before the letters *e, i,* or *y*, it usually makes the sound /j/ (germ).

No word ends with the letter *v*. The *v* is always followed by a silent *e* (give).

No word ends with the letter *j*. The sound /j/ at the end of a word is spelled *-ge* (large) or *-dge* (fudge).

No word ends with the letter *i* (except for some words of foreign derivation, such as *spaghetti* or *ski*). When a word ends with the sound /i/, it is spelled with the letter *y* (fly).

The letter *q* is always followed by a *u,* and the *qu* says /kw/ (quiet).

The letter *y* at the start of a word or syllable makes its consonant sound /y/ (yellow). When *y* does not come at the start of a word or syllable, it is a vowel. It may say /ē/ (happy), /ī/ (cry), or /ĭ/ (gym).

The regular sound of the letter *x* is /ks/, and it usually comes at the end of a word or syllable (fox).

Silent *e* Rules

There are five kinds of silent *e*'s.

The silent *e* that changes the preceding vowel from short to long, sometimes called magic *e* (can/cane).

The silent *e* that is needed because no word can end with a *v* (have).

The silent *e* that is needed to make a *c* or *g* say its soft sound (dance, charge).

The silent *e* that is added to special syllable endings because every syllable has to have a vowel (bubble).

The silent *e* that is added to words that are not plural, so they do not end with a single *s* (horse).

Short Vowel Rules

The short vowel rules apply only to one-syllable words. They are based on the principle that a short vowel must have an extra letter to lean on.

The consonants *l, f, s,* and *z* are doubled after a short vowel (well, stiff, kiss, jazz).

The sound /k/ is spelled -*ck* after a short vowel (pack). Otherwise it is spelled *k* (park).

The sound /j/ is spelled -*dge* after a short vowel (fudge). Otherwise it is spelled -*ge* (charge).

The sound /ch/ is spelled -*tch* after a short vowel (catch). Otherwise it is spelled *ch* (lunch).

In a word with a special syllable ending, the medial consonant is doubled after a short vowel (giggle).

In root words of two syllables, the medial consonant is usually doubled after a short vowel (rabbit).

Rules for Adding Suffixes

The Silent *e* Rule
When adding a suffix to a word ending with silent *e*, drop the *e* before a vowel suffix (hoping). Do not drop the *e* before a consonant suffix (hopeful).

Doubling Rule
In a one-syllable word ending with one vowel followed by one consonant, double the consonant before a vowel suffix (shipped). Do not double the consonant before a consonant suffix (shipment).

The *Y* Rule
In a word ending with a consonant followed by the letter *y,* change the *y* to *i* before adding a suffix (tried). Do not, however, change the *y* if the suffix already begins with an *i* (trying).

Rules for Reading Multisyllable Words

The purpose of teaching the types of syllables and rules for syllable division is to give students strategies for determining the vowel sounds when reading unfamiliar words.

Six Types of Syllables

An **open** syllable ends with a vowel, and the vowel sound is usually long (no, ze-ro).

A **closed** syllable ends with a consonant, and the vowel, sound is short (not, rab-bit).

An **r-controlled** syllable contains a vowel followed by the letter *r*, which controls the sound of the vowel (star, bar-ber).

A **silent-e** syllable ends with a silent *e*, which makes the vowel sound long (note, com-plete).

A **vowel team** syllable contains two vowels that make one sound (join, main-tain).

A **special syllable ending** contains a consonant followed by the letters *le*. It is the only syllable type that has no vowel sound (which is why it is special) and is only found at the end of multisyllable root words (mar-ble).

Three Rules for Syllable Division

If there are two consonants between the vowels **(VCCV)**, divide between them.

con/test	sud/den	nap/kin

If there is one consonant between the vowels **(VCV)**, try dividing after the vowel.

ho/tel	be/gin	ro/bot

If that does not produce a recognizable word, divide after the consonant.

hab/it	lim/it	riv/er

If three consonants are between the vowels **(VCCCV)**, try dividing after the first consonant.

com/plete	chil/dren	hun/dred

If that does not produce a recognizable word, divide after the second consonant.

part/ner	pump/kin	ang/ry

Materials

You can order the materials at **PAFprogram.com**

Getting Started

If you are planning to implement PAF with students who are beginning formal reading instruction, start PAF at Level 1. You will need the following materials:

> 1 Alphabet Picture Cards
>
> 1 Pocket Chart Alphabet
>
> 1 Review Pack 1

And for each child:

> 1 First Steps in Reading
>
> 1 Stepping Up in Reading – Book 1
>
> 1 Handwriting Program for Print
>
> 1 Merrill Reader A - *I Can*
>
> 1 Merrill Skills Book A - *I Can*
>
> 1 PAF Reading Series Book 1- *Pals*

If you are planning to use PAF remedially, we recommend you download the *PAF Placement Test* to determine at which level to begin. The charts below will tell you which materials are used at different levels.

Materials by Level
Levels 1-96

Merrill Readers and Skills Books	Book A *(I Can)* Book B *(Dig In)* Book C *(Catch On)* Book D *(Get Set)*
Stepping Up in Reading Books	First Steps In Reading Stepping Up In Reading I
Handwriting Books	Handwriting Program for Print Handwriting Program for Numerals
Card Packs	Alphabet Picture Cards Pocket Chart Alphabet Cards Review Pack I Key Word Picture Cards

Levels 97-158

Merrill Readers and Skills Books	Book E *(Step Up)* Book F *(Lift Off)*
Stepping Up in Reading	Stepping Up In Reading 2
Card Packs	Review Pack I Review Pack II Key Word Picture Cards

Levels 159-215

Merrill Readers and Skills Books	Book G *(Take Flight)* Book H *(Break Through)*
Stepping Up in Reading	Stepping Up In Reading 3

Handwriting Books	Handwriting Program for Cursive
	    Right Handed
	    Left Handed

Card Packs	Review Pack II Key Word Picture Cards Cursive Wall Strip
Chapter Books	Hannah Absolutely Lucy The Chalk Box Kid The Paint Brush Kid

Material by Category

Stepping Up in Reading Books First Steps In Reading Stepping Up In Reading 1 Stepping Up In Reading 2 Stepping Up In Reading 3	**Merrill Readers** Book A *I Can* Book B *Dig In* Book C *Catch On* Book D *Get Set* Book E *Step Up* Book F *Lift Off* Book G *Take Flight* Book H *Break Through*
Handwriting Books Handwriting Program for Print Handwriting Program for Cursive (RH) Handwriting Program for Cursive (LH) Handwriting Program for Numerals	**Merrill Skills Books** Book A *I Can* Book B *Dig In* Book C *Catch On* Book D *Get Set* Book E *Step Up* Book F *Lift Off* Book G *Take Flight* Book H *Break Through*
Card Packs Alphabet Picture Cards Review Pack I Review Pack II Pocket Chart Alphabet Key Word Picture Cards Cursive Wall Strip Cursive Alphabet Picture Cards	**PAF Reading Series** Book 1 *Pals* Book 2 *Fun in the Sun* Book 3 *Let's Go*

Writing Papers

Levels 1-74 **Books A-C**	½" ruled Skip Line Paper (085215)	School Specialty schoolspecialty.com 888-388-3224
Levels 75-96 **Books D-E**	3/8" ruled Skip Line Paper (085216)	School Specialty schoolspecialty.com 888-388-3224
Levels 97-215 **Books F-H**	3/16" ruled Single Sheets (6037) Composition Book (2537)	Becker's School Supplies shopbecker.com 800-523-1490

PAF Reading Series

The PAF Reading Series is a new set of decodable readers being developed by the authors of the PAF program. The readers follow the PAF Instructional Sequence and can be used in place of the Merrill Readers or for additional decodable text.

YOU CAN USE THE READERS AT THE FOLLOWING LEVELS

Levels 1 - 33   Book 1

Pals

Levels 34 - 52  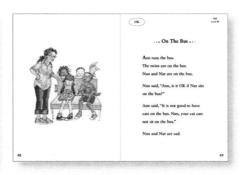 Book 2

Fun in the Sun

Levels 53- 74   Book 3

Let's Go

Levels 75-96 **Book 4** *Camp Hilltop*
Levels 97-129 **Book 5** *Stand by Me* **coming soon!**

Books 6, 7 & 8 (levels 130-215) **to follow.**

For more information or to order, please go to **pafprogram.com**
or email **customer.service@pafprogram.com.**

BIBLIOGRAPHY

Dyslexia and Learning Disabilities

Catts, Hugh, and Alan Kahmi. <u>Language and Reading Disabilities</u>. Boston, MA: Allyn and Bacon, 2012.

Gabrieli, John. "Dyslexia: A New Synergy Between Education and Cognitive Neuroscience." <u>Science</u> 325.5938 (July 2009): 280-283.

Gillingham, Anna, and Bessie Stillman. <u>Remedial Training for Children with Specific Disability in Reading, Spelling and Penmanship</u>. Cambridge, MA: Educators Publishing Service, 1997.

Henry, Marcia. "Structured, Multisensory Teaching: The Orton Legacy." <u>Annals of Dyslexia</u> 58.1 (1998): 3-26.

Lyon, G. Reid. "Toward a Definition of Dyslexia." <u>Annals of Dyslexia</u> 45.1 (1995): 3-27.

Morris, Robin. "Reflections on Transition in the Field of Dyslexia: Learning from the Past to Benefit the Future." <u>Unraveling Reading Comprehension</u>. Eds. Brett Miller, Laurie Cutting, and Peggy McCardle. Baltimore, MD: Brooks Publishing, 2013. 8-19.

Pennington, Bruce. <u>Diagnosing Learning Disabilities: A Neuropsychological Framework</u>. New York: The Guilford Press, 2010.

Shaywitz, Sally. "Dyslexia." <u>The New England Journal of Medicine</u> 338.5 (1998): 307-312.

---. <u>Overcoming Dyslexia: A New and Complete Science-Based Program for Reading Problems at Any Level</u>. New York: Alfred A. Knopf, 2003.

Seidenberg, Mark. <u>Language at the Speed of Light</u>. New York:Perseus Books, 2017.

Westby, Carol. "Beyond Decoding: Critical and Dynamic Literacy for Students with Dyslexia, Language Learning Disabilities or Attention Deficit-Hyperactivity Disorder." <u>Speaking, Reading and Writing in Children with Language Learning Disabilities</u>. Eds. Katharine Butler, and Elaine Silliman. Mahwah, NJ: Lawrence Erlbaum Associates, 2002. 73-107.

---. <u>Dyslexia, Fluency and the Brain</u>. Timonium, MD: York Press, 2001.

Teaching Reading

Adams, Marilyn. <u>Beginning to Read: Thinking and Learning About Print</u>. Cambridge, MA: MIT Press, 1998.

Badian, Nathlie. <u>Prediction and Prevention of Reading Failure.</u> Timonium, MD: York Press, 2000.

Beck, Isabel, and Connie Juel. "The Role of Decoding in Learning to Read." <u>American Educator</u> 19.2 (1995): 21-25, 39-42.

Brady, Susan A. "Efficacy of Phonics Teaching for Reading Outcomes: Indications from Post-NRP Research." <u>Explaining Individual Differences in Reading.</u> Eds. Susan A. Brady, David Braze and Carol A. Fowler. New York, NY: Psychology Press, 2011. 69-86.

Chall, Jeanne. <u>Learning to Read: The Great Debate</u>. New York: McGraw Hill, 1983.

---. <u>Stages of Reading Development</u>. New York: Harcourt Brace College Publishers, 1996.

Christense, Carol, and Judith Bowey. "The Efficacy of Orthographic Rime, Grapheme-Phoneme Correspondence and Implicit Phonics Approaches to Teaching Decoding Skills." <u>Scientific Studies of Reading</u> 9.4 (2005): 327-349.

Ehri, Linnea. "Orthographic Mapping in theAcquisition of Sight Word Reading, Spelling, Memory and Vocabulary Learning." <u>Scientific Studies of Reading</u>. 18.1 (2014): 5-21.

Ehri, Linnea, Simone R. Nunes, Steven A. Stahl, and Dale M. Willows. "Systematic Phonics Instruction Helps Students Learn To Read: Evidence from the National Reading Panel's Meta-Analysis." <u>Review of Educational Research</u> 71.3 (2001): 393-447.

Foorman, Barbara. ed. <u>Preventing and Remediating Reading Difficulties: Bringing Science to Scale</u> Timonium, MD: York Press 2003.

Foorman, Barbara, and Joseph Torgesen. "Critical Elements of Classroom and Small-Group Instruction Promote Reading Success in All Children." <u>Learning Disabilities Research & Practice</u> 16.4 (2001): 203-212.

Johnston, Rhona S. and Joyce Watson. "Accelerating the Development of Reading, Spelling and Phonemic Awareness Skills in Initial Readers." <u>Reading and Writing</u> 17.4 (2004): 327-357.

Lyon, G. Reid, and Vinita Chhabra. "The Science of Reading Research." <u>Educational Leadership</u> 61.6 (March 2004): 12-17.

McCardle, Peggy, and Vinita Chhabra, eds. <u>The Voice of Evidence in Reading Research</u>. Baltimore, MD: Brooks Publishing, 2004.

McCardle, Peggy, Vinita Chhabra, and Barbara Kapinus, eds. <u>Reading Research in Action</u>. Baltimore, MD: Brooks Publishing, 2008.

Moats, Louisa. "Teaching Decoding." <u>American Educator</u> 22.1 (1998): 1-9.

Nunes, Terezinha, Peter Bryant and Rossana Barros. "The Development of Word Recognition and Its Significance for Comprehension and Fluency." http://dx.doi.org/10.1037/a0027412, 2012.

Patton, Susannah, and Madelyn Holmes. <u>The Keys to Literacy</u>. Washington, D.C. Council for Basic Education, 2002.

Pugh, Ken and Peggy McCardle . <u>How Children Learn to Read</u>. New York, NY: Psychology Press, 2009.

Rayner, Keith, Barbara Foorman, Charles Perfetti, David Pesetsky, and Mark Seidenberg. "How Psychological Science Informs the Teaching of Reading." <u>Psychological Science in the Public Interest</u> 2.2 (2001): 31-74.

<u>Report of the National Reading Panel - An Evidence-Based Assessment of the Scientific Research Literature on Reading and Its Implications for Reading Instruction</u>. April 2000. www.nationalreadingpanel.org.

Stanovich, Keith. "Matthew Effect in Reading: Some Consequences of Individual Differences in the Acquisition of Literacy." Reading Research Quarterly 21.4 (1986): 360-406.

Teaching Reading Is Rocket Science. Washington D.C.: American Federation of Teachers, 1999.

Torgesen, Joseph K. "Preventing Early Reading Failure - Avoiding the Devastating Downward Spiral." American Educator 8.3 (2004): 7-19.

United States. National Academy of Educators. Becoming a Nation of Readers The Report of the Commission of Reading. Washington D.C., 1985.

United States. National Institute for Literacy. National Reading Panel. Put Reading First – The Research Building Blocks for Teaching Children to Read. www.nationalreadingpanel.org/publications/researchread.htm, 2006.

Reading Fluency

Bashir, Anthony, and Pamela Hook. "Fluency: A Key Link Between Word Identification and Comprehension." Language Speech Hearing Services in School. 40.2 (2009): 196-200.

Beach, Kristen and Rollanda O'Connor. "Developing and Strengthening Reading Fluency and Comprehension of Poor Readers in Elementary School: A Focused Review of Research." Perspectives on Language and Literacy. International Dyslexia Association (2014):17-19.

Catts, Hugh, Matthew Gillispie, Laurence Leonard, Robert Kail, and Carol Miller. "The Role of Speed of Processing, Rapid Naming, and Phonological Awareness in Reading Achievement." Journal of Learning Disabilities 35.6 (2002): 510-525.

Chard, David, Sharon Vaughn, and Brenda-Jean Tyler. "A Synthesis of Research on Effective Interventions for Building Reading Fluency with Elementary Students with Learning Disabilities." Journal of Learning Disabilities 35.5 (2002): 386-406.

Hasbrouk, Jan, and Gerald Tindal. "Oral Reading Fluency Norms: A Valuable Assessment Tool for Reading Teachers." The Reading Teacher 59.7 (2006): 636-643.

Hiebert, Elfrieda and Charles Fisher. "A Review of the National Reading Panel's Studies on Fluency: The Role of Text." The Elementary School Journal 105.5 (2005): 443-460.

Hudson, Roxanne. "Fluency Problems: When, Why, and How to Intervene." Handbook of Reading Interventions. Eds. Rolland O'Connor and Patricia Vadasy. New York: Guildford Press, (2011): 169-197.

Juel, Connie and Cecilia Minden-Cupp. "Learning to Read Words: Linguistic Units and Instructional Strategies." Theoretical Models and Processes of Reading. Eds. Robert Ruddell and Norman Unrau. International Reading Association, Newark, DE. 2004.

Katzir, Tami, Youngsuk Kim, Maryanne Wolf, Beth O'Brien, Becky Kennedy, Maureen Lovett and Robin Morris. "Reading Fluency: The Whole is More Than the Parts." Annals of Dyslexia 56.1 (2006): 51-82.

Klauda, Susan and John Guthrie. "Relationships of Three Components of Reading Fluency to Reading Comprehension." Journal of Educational Psychology 100.2 (2008):310-321.

Kuhn, Melanie, Paula Schwanenflugel, Deborah Woo, Elizabeth Meisinger, Rose Sevcik, Barbara Bradley and Steven Stahl. "Teaching Children to Become Fluent and Automatic Readers." Journal of Literacy Research. 38.4 (2006): 357-387.

Nunes, Terezinha, Peter Bryant and Rossana Barros. "The Development of Word Recognition and Its Significance for Comprehension and Fluency." Journal of Educational Psychology 104.4 (2012): 959-971.

O'Connor, Rollanda, Annika White, and H. Lee Swanson. "Repeated Reading Versus Continuous Reading: Influences on Reading Fluency and Comprehension." Exceptional Children 74:1 (2007): 31-46.

Schwanenflugel, Paula, Elizabeth Meisinger, Joseph Wisenbaker, Melanie Kuhn, Gregory Strauss, and Robin Morris. "Becoming a Fluent and Automatic Reader in the Early Elementary Years." Reading Research Quarterly 41.4 (2006): 496-522.

Torgesen, Joseph and Roxanne Hudson. Reading Fluency: Critical Issues for Struggling Readers. Reading Fluency: The Forgotten Dimension of Reading Success. Eds. S. Jay Samuels and Alan Farstrip. International Reading Association, 2006. Newark, DE. 130-158.

Wolf, Maryanne and Tami Katzer-Cohen. "Reading Fluency and Its Intervention." Scientific Studies of Reading. 5.3 (2001): 211-239.

Reading Comprehension

Cain, Kate. "Reading Comprehension Difficulties in Struggling Readers." Unraveling Reading Comprehension. Eds. Brett Miller, Laurie Cutting, and Peggy McCardle. Baltimore, MD:Brooks Publishing. (2013):54-65.

Cain, Kate and Jane Oakhill. Children's Comprehension Problems in Oral and Written Language: A Cognitive Perspective. New York: Guilford Press, 2007.

Carlisle, Joanne and Melinda Rice. Improving Reading Comprehension: Research-Based Principles and Practices. Timonium, MD: York Press, 2002.

Catts, Hugh. "Oral Language Disorders and Reading Comprehension Problems." Unraveling Reading Comprehension. Eds. Brett Miller, Laurie Cutting, and Peggy McCardle. Baltimore, MD:Brooks Publishing, (2013):66-77.

Helder, Anne, Paul Van den Broek, Linda Van Leijenhorst and Katinka Beker "Sources of Comprehension Problems During Reading." Unraveling Reading Comprehension. Eds. Brett Miller, Laurie Cutting, and Peggy McCardle. Baltimore, MD: Brooks Publishing, (2013) 43-53.

Hirsch, E. D., Jr. The Knowledge Deficit. New York: Houghton Mifflin, 2006.

---. "Reading Comprehension Requires Knowledge of Words and the World." American Educator 27.1 (2003): 10-29.

---. "Overcoming the Language Gap: Make Better Use of the Literacy Time Block." American Educator 25.2 (2001): 4-7.

Klauda, Susan, and John Guthrie. "Relationships of Three Components of Reading Fluency to Reading Comprehension." Journal of Educational Psychology 100.2 (2008): 310-321.

Maria, Katherine. Reading Comprehension Instruction: Issues and Strategies. Parkton, MD: York Press, 1990.

Scott, Cheryl. "A Case for the Sentence in Reading Comprehension." Language, Speech and Hearing Services in Schools 40 (April 2009): 184-191.

Stahl, Steven, Victoria Hare, Richard Sinatra, and James Gregory. "Defining the Role of Prior Knowledge and Vocabulary in Reading Comprehension." Journal of Reading Behavior 23:4 (1991): 487-508.

Torgesen, Joseph K. "How Knowledge Helps – It Speeds and Strengthens Reading Comprehension, Learning and Thinking." American Educator 30.1 (2006): 30-38.

Willingham, Daniel. "The Usefulness of Brief Instruction in Reading Comprehension Strategies." American Educator 31.4 (2007): 39-50.

Tong, Xiuli, S. Hélène Deacon, John Kirby, Kate Cain, and Rauno Parrila. "Morphological Awareness: A Key to Understanding Poor Reading Comprehension in English." Journal of Educational Psychology 103.3 (2011): 523-534.

Spelling/Handwriting

Berninger, Virginia. "Educating Students in the Computer Age to be Multilingual by Hand." Invited Commentary on "The Handwriting Debate" NASBE Policy Debate (2012, September) for National Association of State Boards of Education (NASBE), Arlington, VA. National Association of State Boards of Education: 19:1 March 2013.

--- "Strengthening the Mind's Eye: The Case for Continued Handwriting Instruction in the 21st Century." Principal. National Association of Elementary School Principals (May/June 2012) 28-31.

Ehri, Linnea. "Learning to Read and Learning to Spell: Two Sides of the Same Coin." Topics in Language Disorders 20.3 (2000): 19-36.

James, Karin Harman. "Sensori-motor Experience Leads to Changes in Visual Processing in the Developing Brain." Developmental Science 13.2 (March 2010): 279-288.

James, Karin and Laura Engelhardt. "The effects of handwriting experience on functional brain development in pre-literate children." Trends in Neuroscience and Education. 1:1 (Dec 2012): 32-42.

Kahmi, Alan, and Linette Hinton. "Explaining Individual Differences in Spelling Ability." Topics in Language Disorders 20.3 (2000): 37-49.

Moats, Louisa C. "How Spelling Supports Reading." American Educator 29.4 (2005/2006): 12-42.

---. Speech to Print: Language Essentials for Teachers. Baltimore, MD: Brooks Publishing Co., 2000.

Perfetti, Charles, Laurence Rieben, and Michel Fayol, eds. Learning To Spell: Research, Theory and Practice Across Language. Mahwah, New Jersey: Lawrence Erlbaum Associates, 1997.

Post, Yolanda, and Suzanne Carreker. "Orthographic Similarity and Phonological Transparency in Spelling." Reading and Writing: An Interdisciplinary Journal 15.3-4 (2002): 317-340.

Schlagal, Bob. "Traditional, Developmental and Structured Language Approaches to Spelling: Review and Recommendations." Annals of Dyslexia 51.1 (2001): 147-176.

Treiman, Rebecca, and Derrick Bourassa. "The Development of Spelling Skill." Topics in Language Disorder 20 (2000) 1-18.

Weiser, Beverly and Patricia Mathes. "Using Encoding Instruction to Improve the Reading and Spelling Performances of Elementary Students at Risk for Literacy Difficulties: A Best-Evidence Synthesis." Review of Educational Research 81.2 (June 2011) 170-200.

INDEX

Red Words are listed on page 224.

Red Words

again, 116
any, 128
are, 58

because, 105
been, 109
build,125
built, 125
buy, 137

come, 84
could, 98

do, 66
does, 111
done, 82
don't, 70

enough, 141

father, 135
friend, 92
from, 63
full, 94

goes, 66

half, 140

island, 146

laugh, 122

many, 128

none, 82

ocean, 145
of, 56
off, 87-88
once, 121
one, 82
only, 115

people, 124
pretty, 114
put, 59

rough, 141

said, 55
says, 108
school, 71
should, 99
some, 83-84
sure, 104

the, 48
their, 101-102
there, 83, 102, 109
they, 59
to, 51, 139
together, 132
tough, 141
two, 139

very, 65

walk, 90
want, 77
was, 61
water, 133
Wednesday, 142
were, 64
what, 81
where, 91
who, 71
woman, 118
women, 118
won't, 70
would, 99

you, 52
your, 52